From Zero to Online Empire:

A Blueprint for Digital Dominance Through Affiliate Marketing and Blogging

Disclaimer

Copyright © by F. A. Ebenezer 2024. All rights reserved.

No part of this publication may be reproduced, stored in a retrieval system, or transmitted in any form or by any means, electronic, mechanical, photocopying, recording or otherwise, without the prior permission of the publisher.

Table of Contents

Disclaimer 2
Table of Contents 3
Introduction 8
   Welcome to the Digital Age 8
   Understanding the Power of the Online Market 9
   The Journey from Zero to Empire 10
Chapter 1: What is Affiliate Marketing? 13
   The Basics of Affiliate Marketing 13
   How Affiliate Marketing Can Generate Passive Income 14
Chapter 2: Blogging as a Business 20
   The Evolution of Blogging 20
   Why Blogging is Essential for Digital Dominance 23
   Integrating Affiliate Marketing with Blogging 26
Chapter 3: Laying the Foundation 30

Choosing Your Niche 30
Importance of Niche Selection 30
How to Identify Profitable Niches 33
Case Studies of Successful Niches 35

Chapter 4: Building Your Brand 40
Developing a Strong Online Presence 40
Crafting a Memorable Brand Identity 43
Building Trust and Credibility in Your Niche. 46

Chapter 5: Setting Up Your Blog 51
Choosing the Right Platform 51
How to Choose the Right Platform: 55
Essential Tools and Plugins for a Successful Blog 56
How to Choose the Right Tools and Plugins:.. 61
Designing Your Blog for Maximum Impact ... 62

Chapter 6: Content is King 69
Creating High-Quality Content 69
The Importance of Value-Driven Content 72

Content Types that Engage and Convert 74
Developing a Content Strategy 78

Chapter 7: SEO Mastery 82
Introduction to Search Engine Optimization ... 82
On-Page and Off-Page SEO Techniques......... 84
Keyword Research and Content Optimization 89

Chapter 8: Building Traffic................................ 94
Leveraging Social Media for Traffic............... 94
Paid Advertising Strategies............................. 97
Collaborations and Guest Blogging 100

Chapter 9: Affiliate Marketing 101................... 104
How to Find and Join Affiliate Programs...... 104
Choosing the Right Products to Promote 108

Chapter 10: Monetizing Through Blogging 114
Diversifying Income Streams....................... 114
Sponsored Posts, Ads, and Other Revenue Sources 117
Creating and Selling Your Own Products 123

Chapter 11: Maximizing Conversion Rates 129

   Crafting Compelling Calls-to-Action 129

   Email Marketing for Conversions 132

   Using Analytics to Refine Your Strategies 135

Chapter 12: Scaling and Automating 139

   Scaling and Automating 139

   Scaling Your Online Business 139

   Expanding Your Content and Reach 140

   Building a Team and Outsourcing 144

   Leveraging Automation Tools 147

   Conclusion 152

Chapter 13: Advanced Affiliate Marketing Techniques 153

   Leveraging Data and Analytics for Growth .. 153

   Exploring Advanced Marketing Channels 158

   Creating High-Converting Funnels 161

   Conclusion 166

Chapter 14: Maintaining Your Online Empire . 167

Long-Term Strategies for Sustained Success 167

Staying Ahead of Industry Trends 171

Avoiding Common Pitfalls 173

Chapter 15: Case Studies and Interviews 177

Success Stories... 177

Interviews with Top Bloggers and Affiliate Marketers 181

Case Studies of Successful Affiliate Marketing Blogs... 185

Lessons Learned from the Pros 189

Chapter 16: Conclusion 193

Your Path to Digital Dominance 193

Recap of Key Strategies and Insights 194

Encouragement for Your Journey Ahead 197

Chapter 17: Appendices 201

Resource List 201

Recommended Tools and Platforms 201

Introduction

Welcome to the Digital Age

We are living in an era where the internet has not just changed the way we communicate, but it has fundamentally transformed how we do business. The Digital Age, characterized by the ubiquitous presence of technology and the internet, offers unprecedented opportunities for individuals and businesses to create, innovate, and thrive. As we embark on this journey together, it's crucial to understand that the internet is not just a tool—it's a platform that levels the playing field, offering anyone with an idea and a bit of determination the chance to build something extraordinary.

This book is your roadmap to navigating this dynamic landscape. Whether you're a complete beginner or someone with some experience in the online world, the principles, strategies, and techniques you'll discover here are designed to help you build a thriving online empire from scratch.

The possibilities are vast, and the barriers to entry are lower than ever before. But, like any journey, success in the digital realm requires the right mindset, tools, and guidance—this is where your transformation begins.

Understanding the Power of the Online Market

The online market is a bustling, ever-evolving ecosystem that operates 24/7, connecting billions of people across the globe. The sheer scale of this market is staggering. Over 4.9 billion people use the internet, and this number continues to grow. With the rise of e-commerce, digital marketing, and social media, the opportunities for entrepreneurs are virtually limitless.

Affiliate marketing and blogging are two of the most powerful and accessible ways to tap into this vast online market. Affiliate marketing allows you to earn commissions by promoting other people's products, while blogging provides a platform to share your knowledge, build an audience, and create a brand.

When combined, these two strategies can create a synergistic effect, multiplying your income potential and enabling you to reach a global audience.

In this section, we'll explore the incredible potential of the online market. You'll learn why now is the perfect time to start building your online presence, and how the tools at your disposal can help you create something truly impactful. The digital market is vast, but it's also highly competitive. To succeed, you'll need to understand its dynamics, identify your niche, and position yourself effectively. We'll cover all of this and more, setting the stage for your journey from zero to digital dominance.

The Journey from Zero to Empire

Building an online empire doesn't happen overnight. It requires careful planning, consistent effort, and a willingness to learn and adapt. The journey from zero to empire is one of growth—both personal and professional.

It's about starting where you are, with the resources you have, and gradually building something that can stand the test of time.

This book is structured to guide you step by step through this journey. We'll start by laying a solid foundation, helping you choose the right niche and build a brand that resonates with your target audience. From there, you'll learn how to create high-quality content, drive traffic to your blog, and monetize your efforts through affiliate marketing and other revenue streams.

As you progress, we'll dive into advanced strategies for scaling your business, automating processes, and ultimately creating a sustainable online empire that generates income even when you're not actively working. You'll hear from successful entrepreneurs who have walked this path before you, gaining insights into their experiences and learning from their successes and failures.

The journey to digital dominance is challenging, but it's also incredibly rewarding.

As you move from zero to empire, you'll not only build financial security but also gain the freedom to live life on your own terms. This is your opportunity to create something lasting—an online empire that reflects your passions, values, and ambitions.

So, are you ready to begin? Let's embark on this journey together and turn your dreams of online success into reality.

Chapter 1: What is Affiliate Marketing?

The Basics of Affiliate Marketing

Affiliate marketing is one of the most popular and accessible ways to earn money online. At its core, affiliate marketing is a performance-based marketing strategy where you, as the affiliate, earn a commission for promoting someone else's product or service. Essentially, you act as a middleman, connecting potential buyers with products or services that suit their needs.

Here's how it works: you sign up for an affiliate program, choose products or services to promote, and then share a unique affiliate link on your blog, social media, or other platforms. When someone clicks on your link and makes a purchase, you earn a commission. It's a win-win situation—the company makes a sale, the customer finds a product they need, and you earn a reward for facilitating the transaction.

The beauty of affiliate marketing lies in its simplicity and scalability.

You don't need to create your own product, handle customer service, or manage inventory. Your primary focus is to drive traffic to the affiliate offers and convert that traffic into sales. As you refine your strategies and expand your reach, your potential to earn increases significantly.

How Affiliate Marketing Can Generate Passive Income

One of the most appealing aspects of affiliate marketing is its potential to generate passive income. Passive income is money that you earn with little to no effort after the initial work has been done. Unlike a traditional job where you trade time for money, affiliate marketing allows you to create income streams that continue to generate revenue long after you've set them up.

Here's how it works: once you've created and published content that includes your affiliate links—such as a blog post, video, or social media post—that content can continue to attract visitors and generate sales over time.

For example, if you write a blog post reviewing a popular product, and it ranks well in search engines, people may continue to find and read your post months or even years later. Every time a reader clicks on your affiliate link and makes a purchase, you earn a commission without having to do any additional work.

To maximize your passive income potential, it's important to focus on creating high-quality, evergreen content that remains relevant over time. Additionally, you can implement strategies like search engine optimization (SEO), email marketing, and social media promotion to drive consistent traffic to your affiliate offers.

While affiliate marketing can be highly lucrative, it's important to note that it does require effort, especially in the beginning. Building a successful affiliate marketing business takes time, consistency, and strategic planning. However, once you've put in the groundwork, the rewards can be substantial, allowing you to earn income while you sleep, travel, or focus on other ventures.

Success Stories to Inspire You

To truly grasp the potential of affiliate marketing, let's look at some real-life success stories that demonstrate what's possible when you commit to this business model.

1. **Pat Flynn – Smart Passive Income** Pat Flynn is one of the most well-known figures in the affiliate marketing world. After being laid off from his job as an architect, Pat started an online business centered around helping others pass a particular exam he had experience with. He monetized his blog through affiliate marketing by recommending relevant products and services to his audience. Today, Pat earns a significant portion of his income from affiliate marketing, and his website, Smart Passive Income, has become a go-to resource for aspiring online entrepreneurs.
2. **Michelle Schroeder-Gardner – Making Sense of Cents** Michelle Schroeder-

Gardner started her blog, Making Sense of Cents, as a personal finance blog to share her journey of paying off student loans. Over time, she began monetizing her blog through affiliate marketing, promoting financial products and services that aligned with her content. Her blog has grown into a thriving business, and Michelle now earns over six figures a month, with a large portion of that income coming from affiliate marketing.

3. **John Chow – JohnChow.com** John Chow is a successful blogger and affiliate marketer who has turned his website, JohnChow.com, into a multi-million-dollar business. He started by sharing tips on making money online and gradually built a loyal audience. John's success in affiliate marketing comes from his ability to create engaging content and effectively promote high-ticket affiliate products. His journey is a testament to the power of affiliate marketing when combined with a strong personal brand.

4. **The Wirecutter – Acquired by The New York Times** The Wirecutter, founded by Brian Lam, started as a simple product review blog. The site focused on providing in-depth reviews of consumer electronics and other products, with affiliate links to retailers like Amazon. The Wirecutter's unbiased, well-researched content attracted a large audience, and the site generated significant affiliate revenue. In 2016, The New York Times acquired The Wirecutter for $30 million, showcasing the enormous potential of affiliate marketing when done right.

These success stories highlight the diversity of paths available in affiliate marketing. Whether you're starting a blog, building a review site, or leveraging your expertise in a specific niche, the possibilities are vast. What these individuals have in common is a commitment to providing value to their audience, a willingness to learn and adapt, and the perseverance to see their efforts through to success.

As you embark on your own affiliate marketing journey, remember that success doesn't come overnight. But with dedication, strategic thinking, and a focus on delivering genuine value to your audience, you too can build a profitable affiliate marketing business that generates passive income and opens the door to financial freedom.

Chapter 2: Blogging as a Business

The Evolution of Blogging

Blogging has come a long way since its humble beginnings in the late 1990s, when it was primarily used as a personal online diary. Back then, blogs were simple, text-heavy websites where individuals shared their thoughts, experiences, and daily activities with a small audience of friends and family. The word "blog" itself is a shortened form of "weblog," reflecting its original purpose as a log of web activity.

Over time, blogging evolved from a niche hobby into a powerful tool for communication, information sharing, and, ultimately, business. As the internet expanded and technology advanced, blogs began to play a significant role in shaping public opinion, influencing purchasing decisions, and even driving political movements. Today, blogging is a multi-billion-dollar industry that has transformed countless individuals and businesses into influential voices in their respective fields.

The evolution of blogging can be seen in several key areas:

1. **Content Diversity:**
   Modern blogs are no longer limited to text. They encompass a wide range of content types, including videos, podcasts, infographics, and interactive media. This evolution has allowed bloggers to reach and engage with a broader audience, catering to different preferences and learning styles.
2. **Professionalism:**
   Blogging has become a serious business, with many bloggers earning full-time incomes from their efforts. This shift has led to increased professionalism in the blogging industry, with a focus on quality content, branding, and strategic marketing. Bloggers are now seen as experts in their niches, often collaborating with brands, publishers, and media outlets.
3. **Monetization:**

The rise of blogging as a business has led to the development of various monetization strategies, including affiliate marketing, sponsored content, advertising, and product sales. Bloggers have learned to leverage their platforms to generate revenue, turning their passion projects into profitable enterprises.

4. **Community Building:** Blogs have become hubs for online communities, where readers can interact with the blogger and with each other. This sense of community has strengthened the relationship between bloggers and their audiences, leading to increased loyalty and engagement.

As blogging continues to evolve, it remains a powerful and versatile platform for sharing information, expressing creativity, and building a business. Whether you're just starting out or looking to take your blog to the next level, understanding the evolution of blogging will help you appreciate its potential and harness its power for your own success.

Why Blogging is Essential for Digital Dominance

In the digital age, having a strong online presence is crucial for anyone looking to establish authority, build an audience, and generate income. Blogging is one of the most effective ways to achieve digital dominance for several reasons:

1. **Content Ownership:** Unlike social media platforms, where you're subject to the whims of algorithms and platform policies, your blog is your own digital real estate. You have full control over the content, design, and monetization strategies, allowing you to create a unique brand identity and experience for your audience.
2. **SEO Benefits:** Blogs are a powerful tool for search engine optimization (SEO). By consistently publishing high-quality, keyword-rich content, you can improve your blog's visibility in search engine results, driving organic traffic to your site.

This not only increases your reach but also positions you as an authority in your niche.

3. **Building Authority and Trust:** A well-maintained blog allows you to showcase your expertise, share valuable insights, and provide solutions to your audience's problems. Over time, this builds trust and credibility, making your blog the go-to resource for information in your niche. As your authority grows, so does your influence, leading to greater opportunities for collaboration, monetization, and brand partnerships.
4. **Engagement and Community Building:** Blogs are an excellent platform for engaging with your audience on a deeper level. Through comments, email newsletters, and social media integration, you can foster a sense of community around your blog, encouraging readers to return regularly, share your content, and participate in discussions. This engagement not only drives traffic but also creates a loyal following that supports your long-term success.

5. **Monetization Opportunities:** Blogging opens up a wide range of monetization opportunities, from affiliate marketing and advertising to selling your own products or services. By building a blog that attracts a targeted audience, you can create multiple income streams, turning your blog into a profitable business. The scalability of blogging means that as your audience grows, so does your earning potential.
6. **Long-Term Impact:** Unlike social media posts that quickly fade into obscurity, blog content has a long shelf life. Evergreen blog posts—those that remain relevant over time—can continue to attract traffic and generate income for years. This long-term impact makes blogging a valuable investment in your digital presence and a key component of your strategy for achieving digital dominance.

Blogging is not just a tool for communication; it's a cornerstone of digital success.

By building and maintaining a blog, you create a platform that amplifies your voice, establishes your authority, and opens up endless opportunities for growth and income generation.

Integrating Affiliate Marketing with Blogging

The synergy between blogging and affiliate marketing is one of the most powerful combinations in the digital world. When done correctly, integrating affiliate marketing with your blog can transform your online presence into a highly profitable venture.

Here's how to effectively integrate affiliate marketing with blogging:

1. **Choosing the Right Affiliate Programs:** The first step is to select affiliate programs that align with your blog's niche and audience. Choose products or services that your readers are likely to be interested in and that you can genuinely recommend. Look for affiliate programs that offer competitive commissions, reliable tracking, and robust support.

2. **Creating Relevant Content:**
Content is the foundation of your blog, and it's also the vehicle for your affiliate marketing efforts. Focus on creating high-quality, value-driven content that naturally incorporates your affiliate links. This could include product reviews, how-to guides, tutorials, and comparison posts. The key is to provide valuable information that helps your readers make informed purchasing decisions.
3. **Incorporating Affiliate Links Strategically:**
Placement of affiliate links is crucial for maximizing conversions. Avoid overwhelming your readers with too many links; instead, integrate them naturally within your content. You can include affiliate links in your blog posts, sidebars, email newsletters, and even within video or podcast content. Make sure to disclose your affiliate relationships transparently to maintain trust with your audience.
4. **Optimizing for SEO:**

To drive traffic to your blog and affiliate offers, focus on optimizing your content for search engines. Conduct keyword research to identify the terms your audience is searching for, and incorporate these keywords into your blog posts. Additionally, focus on building backlinks, improving site speed, and enhancing the user experience to boost your blog's search engine rankings.

5. **Using Analytics to Refine Your Strategy:** Monitoring the performance of your affiliate marketing efforts is essential for success. Use analytics tools to track metrics such as click-through rates, conversion rates, and revenue generated from affiliate links. This data will help you understand what's working and where improvements can be made. By continuously refining your strategy based on data-driven insights, you can maximize your affiliate marketing income.
6. **Building a Loyal Audience:**

Successful affiliate marketing is built on trust. By consistently delivering valuable content and maintaining an authentic connection with your audience, you can build a loyal following that values your recommendations. This loyalty translates into higher conversion rates and repeat purchases, ultimately boosting your affiliate marketing revenue.

By integrating affiliate marketing with your blog, you create a powerful engine for generating passive income. Your blog serves as the platform for attracting and engaging your audience, while affiliate marketing provides the monetization strategy that turns your content into cash. Together, these elements form the foundation of your online empire, positioning you for digital dominance in your niche.

Chapter 3: Laying the Foundation

Choosing Your Niche

Selecting the right niche is one of the most critical decisions you'll make when building your online empire through blogging and affiliate marketing. Your niche is the specific area or topic that your blog will focus on, and it will determine the type of content you create, the audience you attract, and the affiliate products you promote. In this chapter, we'll explore the importance of niche selection, how to identify profitable niches, and examine case studies of successful niches that have led to thriving online businesses.

Importance of Niche Selection

Choosing the right niche sets the foundation for your entire online business. Here's why niche selection is so crucial:

1. **Focus and Clarity:**

A well-defined niche helps you focus your efforts and provides clarity on the type of content you should create. It's much easier to build an audience and establish yourself as an authority when you're focused on a specific topic rather than trying to cover everything. Your readers will know exactly what to expect from your blog, which builds trust and loyalty.

2. **Audience Targeting:** By choosing a niche, you can tailor your content to meet the specific needs and interests of a targeted audience. This not only makes it easier to attract readers but also increases the likelihood of conversions when promoting affiliate products. A targeted audience is more engaged, more likely to share your content, and more likely to purchase through your affiliate links.
3. **Monetization Potential:** Not all niches are created equal when it comes to monetization. Some niches have higher demand, better affiliate programs, and more lucrative opportunities.

By carefully selecting a niche with strong monetization potential, you position yourself for greater success in generating income from your blog.

4. **Competitive Advantage:**
   A well-chosen niche allows you to stand out in a crowded market. Instead of competing with millions of generalist blogs, you can carve out a unique space where you can establish yourself as an expert. This competitive advantage can lead to higher search engine rankings, more traffic, and greater influence in your niche.
5. **Sustainability:**
   Passion and interest in your niche are key factors in sustaining your blog over the long term. Building a successful blog requires consistent effort, and it's much easier to stay motivated and produce quality content when you're genuinely interested in the topic. A niche that aligns with your passions and expertise is more likely to result in long-term success.

How to Identify Profitable Niches

Identifying a profitable niche requires a combination of research, introspection, and strategic thinking. Here's a step-by-step guide to help you find the right niche for your blog:

1. **Assess Your Interests and Expertise:** Start by brainstorming topics that you're passionate about and knowledgeable in. Your niche should align with your interests, as this will make it easier to create content and engage with your audience. Additionally, consider your unique skills and experiences—these can give you an edge in your chosen niche.
2. **Research Market Demand:** Once you've identified potential niches, research their market demand. Use tools like Google Trends, keyword research tools, and social media platforms to gauge the popularity of your chosen topics. Look for niches that have a steady or growing interest over time.

High search volume for related keywords is a good indicator of strong demand.

3. **Analyze the Competition:** Evaluate the competition within your potential niches. A niche with too much competition may be difficult to break into, while a niche with too little competition may indicate a lack of demand. Look for niches with a moderate level of competition—this suggests that there's demand, but still room for a new player to make an impact.
4. **Explore Monetization Opportunities:** Not all niches are equally profitable. Investigate the affiliate programs, products, and services available within your potential niches. Are there high-quality products that you can promote? What are the commission rates like? Consider whether the niche offers multiple revenue streams, such as digital products, courses, or memberships.
5. **Evaluate Longevity:** Choose a niche with staying power.

Trends come and go, but evergreen topics that remain relevant over time are more likely to provide long-term income. Consider whether your chosen niche will still be relevant and profitable in the years to come.

6. **Test Your Ideas:** Before committing fully to a niche, test your ideas. You can create a few blog posts, run small ad campaigns, or engage with potential audiences on social media to gauge interest. This will give you a sense of how well your content resonates with your target audience and whether there's potential for growth.

Case Studies of Successful Niches

To illustrate the process of choosing a profitable niche, let's look at some case studies of successful niches that have led to thriving online businesses:

1. **Personal Finance – Making Sense of Cents by Michelle Schroeder-Gardner:**

Michelle Schroeder-Gardner started her blog, *Making Sense of Cents,* as a personal finance blog focused on budgeting, saving, and paying off debt. Her blog resonated with a large audience of readers looking to improve their financial situation. By promoting financial products and services through affiliate marketing, Michelle was able to turn her blog into a six-figure business. The personal finance niche has proven to be highly profitable, with endless opportunities for content creation and affiliate marketing.

2. **Health and Fitness – Nerd Fitness by Steve Kamb:**
Steve Kamb founded *Nerd Fitness,* a blog that caters to people who want to get in shape but might feel intimidated by traditional fitness culture. By targeting a specific audience—self-proclaimed "nerds" who are interested in fitness—Steve carved out a unique niche in the crowded health and fitness market.

Through affiliate marketing, online courses, and a strong community, *Nerd Fitness* has grown into a thriving business. The health and fitness niche is evergreen and offers numerous monetization opportunities.

3. **Parenting and Family – Scary Mommy by Jill Smokler:** Jill Smokler started *Scary Mommy* as a personal blog about her experiences as a mother. Over time, the blog expanded to cover a wide range of topics related to parenting and family life. *Scary Mommy* became a go-to resource for parents, and its success led to monetization through affiliate marketing, sponsored content, and ad revenue. The parenting niche is vast and always in demand, making it a lucrative choice for bloggers.
4. **Travel – The Blonde Abroad by Kiersten Rich:** Kiersten Rich, the founder of *The Blonde Abroad,* turned her passion for travel into a successful blog.

By focusing on solo female travel, Kiersten was able to tap into a specific audience with unique needs and interests. Her blog offers travel guides, tips, and affiliate product recommendations, generating income through affiliate marketing and partnerships. The travel niche is highly competitive, but by narrowing her focus to solo female travelers, Kiersten found a profitable sub-niche with less competition.

5. **Digital Marketing – Smart Passive Income by Pat Flynn:** Pat Flynn's blog, *Smart Passive Income,* focuses on helping people build online businesses and generate passive income. Pat shares his own experiences, case studies, and income reports, providing valuable insights to his audience. Through affiliate marketing, digital products, and courses, *Smart Passive Income* has become one of the most successful blogs in the digital marketing niche. The demand for digital marketing knowledge continues to grow, making it a highly profitable niche.

These case studies demonstrate that success in blogging and affiliate marketing often comes from identifying a specific audience, understanding their needs, and providing valuable content that meets those needs. By carefully selecting a niche that aligns with your interests, has strong demand, and offers monetization opportunities, you can lay a solid foundation for building your online empire.

Choosing your niche is the first step on your journey to digital dominance. Take the time to research, plan, and evaluate your options, and you'll be well on your way to creating a blog that not only resonates with your audience but also generates significant income.

Chapter 4: Building Your Brand

In the digital landscape, your brand is your identity. It's what sets you apart from the countless other blogs and businesses vying for attention online. Building a strong brand is essential for establishing your authority, attracting a loyal audience, and driving your business's long-term success. In this chapter, we'll explore how to develop a strong online presence, craft a memorable brand identity, and build trust and credibility in your niche.

Developing a Strong Online Presence

Your online presence is the sum of all your activities on the internet—your website, social media profiles, content, and interactions with your audience. Developing a strong online presence is crucial for reaching your target audience and establishing your brand as a leader in your niche. Here's how to do it:

1. Create a Professional Website:

Your website is the cornerstone of your online presence. It's where potential readers, customers, and collaborators will go to learn more about you and your brand. Invest in a professional, user-friendly website that reflects your brand's identity. Ensure your website is mobile-friendly, fast-loading, and easy to navigate. Include essential pages such as an About page, Contact page, and Blog.

2. **Leverage Social Media:** Social media platforms are powerful tools for expanding your reach and engaging with your audience. Choose platforms that align with your niche and where your target audience is most active. Regularly post content that resonates with your audience, and engage with them through comments, likes, shares, and direct messages. Social media can also be used to drive traffic to your website and promote your affiliate products.
3. **Consistency is Key:** Consistency in your online activities is vital for building a recognizable brand.

This means posting content regularly, maintaining a consistent tone and style across all platforms, and staying active in your community. Consistency helps build trust with your audience and ensures that your brand remains top-of-mind.

4. **Engage with Your Audience:** Building a strong online presence isn't just about broadcasting your message—it's also about listening and interacting. Respond to comments on your blog and social media, participate in online discussions, and show appreciation for your audience's support. Engaging with your audience fosters a sense of community and loyalty, which are critical for long-term success.
5. **Optimize for Search Engines:** Search engine optimization (SEO) is crucial for increasing your visibility online. By optimizing your website and content for relevant keywords, you can improve your rankings in search engine results, making it easier for potential readers and customers to find you.

SEO involves both on-page factors, such as keyword usage and meta descriptions, and off-page factors, such as backlinks and social signals.

6. **Collaborate and Network:** Networking with other bloggers, influencers, and businesses in your niche can significantly boost your online presence. Collaborations, guest posts, and partnerships allow you to tap into new audiences and build valuable relationships within your industry. Networking also enhances your credibility and can lead to new opportunities for growth.

Crafting a Memorable Brand Identity

Your brand identity is the visual, emotional, and conceptual representation of your brand. It's what people think of when they hear your brand name or see your logo. Crafting a memorable brand identity is crucial for standing out in your niche and creating a lasting impression. Here's how to create a brand identity that resonates with your audience:

1. **Define Your Brand's Mission and Values:**

Your brand's mission and values are the foundation of your identity. What do you stand for? What impact do you want to have on your audience or industry? Clearly define your mission and values, and ensure that they are reflected in everything you do—from your content to your customer interactions. A strong mission and set of values will help you connect with your audience on a deeper level.

2. **Choose Your Brand's Voice and Tone:** Your brand's voice and tone are how you communicate with your audience. Are you formal or casual? Playful or serious? Inspirational or educational? Your voice and tone should align with your brand's personality and resonate with your target audience. Consistency in voice and tone across all platforms will help reinforce your brand identity.
3. **Design Your Visual Identity:** Your visual identity includes your logo, color scheme, typography, and overall design aesthetic.

These elements should be consistent across your website, social media, and any other materials you produce. A strong visual identity makes your brand instantly recognizable and helps create an emotional connection with your audience. Consider working with a professional designer to create a logo and visual assets that represent your brand's personality and values.

4. **Create a Memorable Tagline:** A tagline is a short, catchy phrase that encapsulates the essence of your brand. It should be memorable, easy to understand, and aligned with your brand's mission. A great tagline can enhance your brand's recognition and leave a lasting impression on your audience.
5. **Develop a Content Strategy:** Your content is a key component of your brand identity. Develop a content strategy that aligns with your brand's mission, values, and goals.

Decide on the types of content you'll produce (e.g., blog posts, videos, podcasts), how often you'll publish, and the topics you'll cover. Your content should consistently reflect your brand's voice, tone, and visual identity.

6. **Stay Authentic:** Authenticity is critical to building a memorable brand identity. Be true to yourself and your brand's values in everything you do. Audiences can quickly spot inauthenticity, and it can erode trust in your brand. Stay genuine in your communication, and focus on building real connections with your audience.

Building Trust and Credibility in Your Niche

Trust and credibility are the cornerstones of any successful brand. Without them, it's difficult to build a loyal audience or generate consistent income through affiliate marketing. Here's how to establish trust and credibility in your niche:

1. **Provide Value-Driven Content:** The most effective way to build trust with your audience is by consistently delivering valuable content. Your content should be informative, actionable, and relevant to your audience's needs. Focus on solving problems, answering questions, and providing insights that help your readers achieve their goals. When your audience sees that you're genuinely interested in helping them, they're more likely to trust you and return to your blog regularly.
2. **Be Transparent:** Transparency is key to building credibility. Be open and honest about your affiliate relationships, business practices, and any potential conflicts of interest. Clearly disclose when you're promoting affiliate products, and only recommend products that you genuinely believe in. Your audience will appreciate your honesty and be more likely to trust your recommendations.
3. **Showcase Your Expertise:**

Establish yourself as an authority in your niche by showcasing your expertise. Share your knowledge, experiences, and successes through in-depth blog posts, case studies, and tutorials. Consider creating free resources, such as eBooks or webinars, to further demonstrate your expertise. When your audience views you as an expert, they're more likely to trust your advice and recommendations.

4. **Engage with Your Audience:** Building trust requires building relationships. Engage with your audience through comments, social media interactions, and email communication. Show that you value their opinions, and be responsive to their questions and feedback. Personalized interactions can go a long way in fostering trust and loyalty.
5. **Consistent Quality:** Consistency in the quality of your content and interactions is crucial for maintaining trust.

Whether it's a blog post, social media update, or email newsletter, always strive to deliver the best possible experience. Inconsistencies or lapses in quality can damage your credibility and make it difficult to regain your audience's trust.

6. **Leverage Social Proof:** Social proof, such as testimonials, reviews, and endorsements, can significantly enhance your credibility. Encourage satisfied readers or customers to share their positive experiences with your brand. Display these testimonials on your website and social media to show potential new readers that others trust and value your content.
7. **Build Long-Term Relationships:** Trust is built over time, so focus on nurturing long-term relationships with your audience. Provide ongoing value, stay true to your brand's mission, and continue engaging with your audience. Over time, these efforts will build a strong foundation of trust and credibility that will support your brand's growth.

Building a strong brand is a multifaceted process that involves developing a compelling online presence, crafting a memorable identity, and earning the trust and loyalty of your audience. By following the strategies outlined in this chapter, you'll be well on your way to creating a brand that not only stands out in your niche but also drives the long-term success of your online empire.

Chapter 5: Setting Up Your Blog

Setting up your blog is a crucial step in building your online empire. This chapter will guide you through the process of choosing the right platform, selecting essential tools and plugins, and designing your blog for maximum impact. By the end of this chapter, you'll have a solid foundation on which to build a successful and visually appealing blog.

Choosing the Right Platform

Selecting the right blogging platform is the first and most important decision you'll make when setting up your blog. The platform you choose will determine your blog's flexibility, customization options, and ease of use. Here's an overview of the most popular blogging platforms and how to choose the right one for your needs:

1. **WordPress.org (Self-Hosted):**
   WordPress.org is the most popular blogging platform in the world, powering over 40% of all websites.

It's a self-hosted platform, which means you'll need to purchase your own domain name and web hosting. However, the benefits of WordPress.org are immense:

- **Customization:** WordPress.org offers thousands of themes and plugins, allowing you to customize your blog's design and functionality to your exact specifications.
- **Control:** You have complete control over your blog's content, appearance, and monetization strategies.
- **Scalability:** WordPress.org is highly scalable, making it suitable for both small blogs and large, complex websites.

Who should use it? If you're serious about building a professional blog with long-term growth potential, WordPress.org is the best choice.

2. **WordPress.com (Hosted):**

WordPress.com is the hosted version of WordPress. It's easier to set up and maintain, as hosting is included, but it comes with some limitations:

- **Customization:** Fewer customization options compared to WordPress.org.
- **Monetization:** Limited monetization options unless you upgrade to a premium plan.
- **Control:** Less control over your content and website.

Who should use it? WordPress.com is a good choice for beginners who want a simple, hassle-free blogging experience without the need for technical knowledge.

3. **Wix:**
Wix is a user-friendly, drag-and-drop website builder that offers blogging capabilities. It's known for its ease of use and visually appealing templates:

- **Customization:** Limited compared to WordPress, but still offers a decent range of design options.

- **Ease of Use:** Extremely easy to use, with no coding skills required.
- **Control:** Limited control over certain aspects of your blog.

Who should use it? Wix is ideal for those who want a quick and easy way to create a visually stunning blog without dealing with technical details.

4. **Squarespace:**

Squarespace is another popular website builder with strong design capabilities. It's known for its beautiful templates and all-in-one platform:
- **Customization:** Limited compared to WordPress.org but offers professional-looking templates.
- **Ease of Use:** Easy to use with a smooth drag-and-drop interface.
- **Control:** Less control over customization and monetization.

Who should use it? Squarespace is a good option for creatives and businesses that want a sleek, professional-looking blog with minimal setup time.

5. **Blogger:**
   Blogger is a free, hosted blogging platform owned by Google. It's easy to set up and use, but comes with significant limitations:
   - **Customization:** Very limited customization options.
   - **Monetization:** Limited monetization features.
   - **Control:** Google owns your content, so you have less control over your blog.

   Who should use it? Blogger is suitable for hobby bloggers or those looking for a completely free platform with basic blogging features.

How to Choose the Right Platform:

- **Consider Your Goals:**

If you're building a blog with the intention of growing it into a full-fledged business, a self-hosted platform like WordPress.org is the best choice. If you're blogging as a hobby or prefer a simpler setup, a hosted platform like WordPress.com or Wix may be sufficient.

- **Budget:** Consider the costs associated with each platform, including hosting fees, premium themes, and plugins. WordPress.org offers the most flexibility but may require a higher initial investment.
- **Technical Skills:** If you're comfortable with technology and want complete control over your blog, WordPress.org is ideal. If you prefer a more user-friendly experience with less technical involvement, platforms like Wix or Squarespace might be better suited.

Essential Tools and Plugins for a Successful Blog

Once you've chosen your platform, the next step is to equip your blog with the tools and plugins necessary for success.

These tools will help you with everything from content creation to SEO, security, and analytics. Here's a list of essential tools and plugins every successful blog should have:

1. **SEO Plugins:**
   - **Yoast SEO (WordPress):** Yoast SEO is a must-have plugin for optimizing your blog posts for search engines. It helps you optimize your content for keywords, manage meta descriptions, and improve overall SEO.
   - **Rank Math (WordPress):** Another powerful SEO plugin, Rank Math offers advanced features like keyword tracking, schema markup, and local SEO.
2. **Analytics Tools:**
   - **Google Analytics:** Google Analytics is a free tool that provides detailed insights into your blog's traffic, audience behavior, and conversion rates.

It's essential for understanding how your blog is performing and where you can make improvements.

- **MonsterInsights (WordPress):** MonsterInsights is a plugin that integrates Google Analytics directly into your WordPress dashboard, making it easier to access and interpret your data.

3. **Security Plugins:**
   - **Wordfence (WordPress):** Wordfence is a popular security plugin that protects your blog from malware, hacking attempts, and other security threats. It includes features like firewall protection, malware scanning, and login security.
   - **Sucuri (WordPress):** Sucuri is another excellent security plugin that offers comprehensive protection against online threats. It includes website monitoring, malware removal, and firewall protection.

4. **Backup Tools:**
    - **UpdraftPlus (WordPress):** UpdraftPlus is a powerful backup plugin that allows you to create and restore backups of your blog. It supports automatic backups to cloud storage services like Dropbox, Google Drive, and Amazon S3.
    - **Jetpack (WordPress):** Jetpack offers a range of features, including site backups, security, and performance optimization. It's a great all-in-one solution for WordPress users.
5. **Social Media Plugins:**
    - **Social Warfare (WordPress):** Social Warfare is a social sharing plugin that allows you to add attractive sharing buttons to your blog posts. It also includes features like social proof and click-to-tweet.
    - **Monarch (WordPress):** Monarch is a flexible social sharing plugin that offers a variety of button styles and placements.

It's a great way to encourage social sharing and increase your blog's reach.

6. **Email Marketing Tools:**
   - **Mailchimp:** Mailchimp is a popular email marketing platform that allows you to create and manage email lists, design newsletters, and automate email campaigns. It's easy to integrate with most blogging platforms.
   - **ConvertKit:** ConvertKit is designed specifically for bloggers and creators, offering advanced features like email automation, segmentation, and landing pages.
7. **Content Creation Tools:**
   - **Grammarly:** Grammarly is a writing assistant that helps you catch grammar and spelling errors, improve your writing style, and ensure your content is polished and professional.
   - **Canva:** Canva is a graphic design tool that allows you to create stunning visuals for your blog posts, social media, and marketing materials.

It's user-friendly and offers a wide range of templates and design elements.

8. **Performance Optimization Tools:**
    - **WP Super Cache (WordPress):** WP Super Cache is a caching plugin that helps speed up your blog by creating static versions of your pages, reducing server load, and improving load times.
    - **Smush (WordPress):** Smush is an image optimization plugin that compresses and optimizes your images without sacrificing quality. This helps reduce page load times and improve overall site performance.

How to Choose the Right Tools and Plugins:

- **Focus on Essentials:** Start with the most essential tools and plugins that will directly impact your blog's performance, security, and SEO. As your blog grows, you can explore additional tools to enhance your content and user experience.

- **Consider Compatibility:** Ensure that the plugins you choose are compatible with your chosen platform and with each other. Some plugins may conflict, causing issues with your blog's functionality.
- **Regular Updates:** Choose tools and plugins that are regularly updated and supported by their developers. This ensures that they remain secure, functional, and compatible with the latest platform updates.

Designing Your Blog for Maximum Impact

Your blog's design plays a crucial role in attracting and retaining visitors. A well-designed blog not only looks professional but also enhances the user experience, making it easier for readers to navigate, find content, and engage with your brand. Here's how to design your blog for maximum impact:

1. **Choose a Clean and Professional Theme:**
    - **Simplicity:** Opt for a clean, minimalist design that prioritizes content over clutter.

Avoid overly complicated layouts or flashy designs that can distract from your message.

- **Responsiveness:** Ensure your theme is responsive, meaning it adjusts seamlessly to different screen sizes, including mobile devices. With a significant portion of web traffic coming from mobile users, responsive design is non-negotiable.
- **Customization:** Choose a theme that allows for customization, so you can tailor the design to match your brand identity. Most platforms offer a variety of free and premium themes that can be easily customized to suit your needs.

2. **Prioritize User Experience (UX):**
   - **Navigation:** Create a clear and intuitive navigation menu that helps users find what they're looking for quickly. Use categories, tags, and search functionality to organize your content.
   - **Readability:** Use fonts that are easy to read, and maintain a consistent font size and spacing throughout your blog.

Break up long blocks of text with headings, subheadings, and bullet points to improve readability.

- **Loading Speed:** Optimize your blog's loading speed by compressing images, using caching plugins, and minimizing the use of heavy scripts. A fast-loading blog not only improves user experience but also boosts your search engine rankings.

3. **Create an Eye-Catching Header and Logo:**
   - **Header:** Your blog's header is the first thing visitors see, so make it visually appealing and informative. Include your logo, tagline, and a clear call-to-action (CTA) if applicable. The header should also be clean and not too cluttered, allowing visitors to quickly understand what your blog is about.
   - **Logo:** Invest in a professional logo that represents your brand identity. Your logo should be simple, memorable, and scalable, meaning it looks good at any size.

4. **Use High-Quality Images and Visuals:**
   - **Stock Photos:** If you're using stock photos, choose high-quality images that align with your brand's style and message. Avoid overly generic or cliché images.
   - **Custom Graphics:** Consider creating custom graphics, infographics, and illustrations to make your content stand out. Tools like Canva or Adobe Spark can help you design visually appealing graphics, even if you don't have professional design skills.
   - **Consistency:** Maintain a consistent visual style throughout your blog, using the same color palette, fonts, and image styles. This consistency helps reinforce your brand identity.
5. **Add Clear Calls-to-Action (CTAs):**
   - **Placement:** Strategically place CTAs throughout your blog to guide readers toward desired actions, such as subscribing to your newsletter, downloading a free resource, or purchasing a product.

Common CTA placements include the end of blog posts, sidebars, and pop-ups.

- **Design:** Use contrasting colors and bold fonts to make your CTAs stand out. The design should draw attention without being overly aggressive or disruptive to the user experience.

6. **Optimize for SEO and Accessibility:**
    - **SEO:** Ensure your blog's design is optimized for search engines by using SEO-friendly URLs, meta tags, and alt text for images. Also, make sure your content is structured with appropriate headings (H1, H2, H3) and includes relevant keywords.
    - **Accessibility:** Design your blog to be accessible to all users, including those with disabilities. This includes using alt text for images, ensuring sufficient color contrast, and providing keyboard navigation options. Accessibility not only broadens your audience but also reflects positively on your brand.

7. **Incorporate Social Sharing Features:**

- **Social Buttons:** Add social sharing buttons to your blog posts to encourage readers to share your content on platforms like Facebook, Twitter, and LinkedIn. This can help increase your blog's reach and drive more traffic.
- **Follow Buttons:** Include social media follow buttons on your blog to grow your social media presence. These can be placed in the header, footer, or sidebar.

8. **Test and Iterate:**
   - **A/B Testing:** Experiment with different design elements, such as CTAs, color schemes, and layouts, to see what resonates best with your audience. Use A/B testing tools to compare the performance of different versions.
   - **User Feedback:** Regularly seek feedback from your audience to identify areas for improvement.

Use surveys, polls, and analytics to understand how users interact with your blog and where you can make enhancements.

By choosing the right platform, equipping your blog with essential tools and plugins, and designing it for maximum impact, you'll create a professional and user-friendly blog that not only attracts visitors but also keeps them coming back. In the next chapter, we'll dive into creating compelling content that will engage your audience and drive your blog's success.

Chapter 6: Content is King

In the digital world, content is the cornerstone of success. It's the driving force that attracts, engages, and converts your audience. Without high-quality content, even the most well-designed blog will struggle to build an audience or generate income. This chapter will explore the importance of value-driven content, the types of content that engage and convert, and how to develop a content strategy that aligns with your goals.

Creating High-Quality Content

High-quality content is the key to building a loyal audience and establishing your blog as a trusted resource in your niche. It's not just about writing well; it's about delivering real value to your readers. Here's how to create content that resonates:

1. Understand Your Audience:

Before you start writing, take the time to understand who your audience is, what they care about, and what problems they're trying to solve. The more you know about your audience, the better you can tailor your content to meet their needs. Consider creating reader personas—fictional representations of your ideal readers—to guide your content creation.

2. **Focus on Quality Over Quantity:** While it's important to publish content regularly, quality should never be sacrificed for quantity. A few well-researched, well-written posts are far more valuable than a large number of mediocre ones. High-quality content is informative, accurate, engaging, and free of errors.
3. **Offer Value:** Value-driven content is content that provides real, tangible benefits to your readers. Whether it's solving a problem, answering a question, or offering new insights, your content should always leave your readers better off than they were before.

Consider what unique perspective or expertise you can bring to your content that others in your niche cannot.

4. **Be Authentic and Transparent:** Authenticity is a key factor in building trust with your audience. Be honest and transparent in your writing, sharing your experiences, successes, and failures. Readers are more likely to connect with and trust a blogger who is genuine and relatable.
5. **Create Evergreen Content:** Evergreen content is content that remains relevant and valuable long after it's published. While timely content (such as news or trends) has its place, evergreen content provides long-term value and continues to attract traffic over time. Examples of evergreen content include how-to guides, tutorials, and in-depth articles on foundational topics in your niche.
6. **Use Engaging Visuals:** Visual elements such as images, infographics, and videos can enhance your content and make it more engaging.

Visuals break up text, illustrate key points, and can make complex information easier to understand. Be sure to use high-quality visuals that are relevant to your content and aligned with your brand's style.

The Importance of Value-Driven Content

Value-driven content is the heart of any successful blog. It's content that provides real, actionable value to your audience, whether it's solving a problem, answering a question, or providing insights that your readers can't find elsewhere. Here's why value-driven content is so important:

1. **Builds Trust and Credibility:** When you consistently deliver value to your readers, you establish yourself as a credible and trustworthy source of information. Over time, this trust translates into loyalty, with readers returning to your blog for more content and recommending it to others.
2. **Encourages Engagement:**

Value-driven content encourages readers to engage with your blog, whether by leaving comments, sharing your posts on social media, or subscribing to your newsletter. Engaged readers are more likely to become long-term followers and customers.

3. **Boosts SEO:**
 High-quality, value-driven content is more likely to rank well in search engines. Search engines prioritize content that is relevant, informative, and useful to users. By focusing on value, you can improve your blog's SEO and attract more organic traffic.
4. **Drives Conversions:**
 Content that offers value is more likely to convert readers into customers. Whether you're promoting affiliate products, selling your own products, or offering services, value-driven content can guide your readers through the buyer's journey and encourage them to take action.

Content Types that Engage and Convert

Not all content is created equal. Different types of content serve different purposes and resonate with different segments of your audience. To maximize engagement and conversions, it's important to diversify your content strategy with a mix of content types. Here are some of the most effective types of content for engaging and converting your audience:

1. **Blog Posts:**
   Blog posts are the backbone of most content strategies. They can cover a wide range of topics, from how-to guides and tutorials to opinion pieces and industry news. Well-written blog posts that offer valuable insights can attract a steady stream of traffic and establish your authority in your niche.
2. **Listicles:**
   Listicles are blog posts structured as lists (e.g., "10 Tips for...," "7 Best...," etc.). They're easy to read, shareable, and often perform well on social media.

Listicles are particularly effective for providing quick, actionable tips or highlighting key points on a topic.

3. **How-To Guides and Tutorials:** How-to guides and tutorials are some of the most valuable types of content you can create. They provide step-by-step instructions on how to accomplish a specific task or solve a problem, making them highly useful to readers. This type of content is often evergreen and can attract traffic for years to come.
4. **Case Studies:** Case studies provide real-world examples of how a product, service, or strategy has been successfully implemented. They offer proof of effectiveness and can be highly persuasive for readers considering a similar approach. Case studies are particularly effective for B2B blogs and those promoting high-ticket products or services.
5. **Product Reviews and Comparisons:**

Product reviews and comparisons help readers make informed purchasing decisions by providing in-depth analysis and unbiased opinions on different products or services. This type of content is particularly effective for affiliate marketing, as it can drive conversions by helping readers choose the best product for their needs.

6. **Interviews and Expert Roundups:** Interviews with industry experts or roundups featuring insights from multiple experts can add credibility to your blog and provide unique perspectives on important topics. This type of content can also attract traffic from the audiences of the experts featured.

7. **Infographics:**
Infographics present information in a visual format, making complex data or concepts easier to understand and more engaging. Infographics are highly shareable and can drive traffic from social media and other platforms. They're also great for building backlinks, as other websites may link to your infographic as a resource.

8. **Videos:**
   Video content is increasingly popular and can be a powerful tool for engaging your audience. Whether it's tutorials, product reviews, or interviews, videos can add a dynamic element to your content strategy. Videos are also highly shareable and can increase your reach on platforms like YouTube and social media.
9. **Ebooks and Whitepapers:**
   Ebooks and whitepapers are longer-form content that provide in-depth analysis or comprehensive guides on a particular topic. They're often used as lead magnets, offering valuable content in exchange for an email address. This type of content can establish your expertise and build your email list.
10. **Webinars and Online Courses:**
    Webinars and online courses allow you to dive deep into a topic and interact with your audience in real time. They're excellent for building authority, generating leads, and even selling products or services.

Webinars and courses can also be repurposed into other types of content, such as blog posts, videos, or ebooks.

Developing a Content Strategy

A well-planned content strategy is essential for consistently creating high-quality content that engages and converts your audience. Your content strategy should align with your overall business goals and be tailored to your target audience. Here's how to develop a content strategy that drives results:

1. **Set Clear Goals:** Before you start creating content, define what you want to achieve with your blog. Are you looking to build brand awareness, generate leads, drive sales, or establish yourself as an authority in your niche? Your content goals will guide your content creation and help you measure success.
2. **Identify Your Target Audience:** Understanding your target audience is crucial for creating content that resonates.

Who are your ideal readers? What are their pain points, interests, and needs? Use this information to tailor your content to their preferences and ensure it provides real value.

3. **Perform Keyword Research:** Keyword research helps you identify the topics and search terms your audience is interested in. Use tools like Google Keyword Planner, Ahrefs, or SEMrush to find relevant keywords and phrases with high search volume and low competition. These keywords should guide your content creation and help improve your blog's SEO.
4. **Plan Your Content Calendar:** A content calendar is a schedule that outlines what content you'll create and when you'll publish it. Planning your content in advance ensures consistency and helps you stay organized. Your content calendar should include a mix of content types and topics that align with your goals and audience interests.
5. **Create Pillar Content:**

Pillar content is in-depth, comprehensive content that covers a broad topic in your niche. It serves as the foundation for your blog and can be broken down into smaller, more specific pieces of content. For example, a pillar post on "The Ultimate Guide to Affiliate Marketing" could be supported by posts on specific aspects of affiliate marketing, such as choosing the right affiliate programs or optimizing your affiliate links.

6. **Optimize for SEO:** SEO is critical for driving organic traffic to your blog. Optimize your content for search engines by including relevant keywords, using meta tags, and structuring your content with headings and subheadings. Also, focus on creating content that answers your audience's questions and provides value, as search engines prioritize high-quality content.
7. **Promote Your Content:** Creating great content is only half the battle; you also need to promote it effectively.

Share your content on social media, send it to your email list, and reach out to influencers or other bloggers in your niche. Consider using paid promotion, such as social media ads or sponsored posts, to increase your content's reach.

8. **Measure and Refine:** Regularly track the performance of your content using analytics tools like Google Analytics or social media insights. Pay attention to metrics such as page views, bounce rate, time on page, and conversions. Use this data to refine your content strategy, focusing on what works and making improvements where needed.

By creating high-quality, value-driven content that engages and converts your audience, you'll build a loyal following and set the foundation for a successful online empire. In the next chapter, we'll explore how to attract traffic to your blog and turn casual readers into dedicated followers and customers.

Chapter 7: SEO Mastery

Search Engine Optimization (SEO) is one of the most critical aspects of building a successful blog and online business. SEO is the process of optimizing your website and content to rank higher in search engine results pages (SERPs), thereby increasing the visibility of your blog and attracting more organic traffic. In this chapter, we will explore the fundamentals of SEO, delve into on-page and off-page SEO techniques, and guide you through the process of keyword research and content optimization.

Introduction to Search Engine Optimization

SEO is an ever-evolving field that requires a deep understanding of how search engines work and what users are looking for. At its core, SEO is about making your website and content more accessible and appealing to both search engines and users.

When done correctly, SEO can significantly boost your blog's traffic, authority, and revenue.

1. **The Importance of SEO:** SEO is crucial for several reasons. First, it helps you reach a broader audience by improving your visibility on search engines like Google. Second, it drives targeted traffic to your blog, meaning the people who find your site through search engines are more likely to be interested in your content or products. Finally, SEO helps establish your blog's credibility and authority, as high-ranking sites are often perceived as more trustworthy.
2. **How Search Engines Work:** Search engines like Google use complex algorithms to determine the relevance and quality of web pages. These algorithms analyze various factors, including the content of the page, the structure of the website, and the number of backlinks pointing to the page. Based on these factors, the search engine ranks pages in its results.

Understanding how these algorithms work is key to mastering SEO.

3. **The Three Pillars of SEO:** SEO can be divided into three main categories: technical SEO, on-page SEO, and off-page SEO. Technical SEO involves optimizing your website's infrastructure to make it easier for search engines to crawl and index your site. On-page SEO focuses on optimizing the content and HTML elements of your pages. Off-page SEO is about building your site's authority and reputation through backlinks and other external factors.

On-Page and Off-Page SEO Techniques

Both on-page and off-page SEO are essential for a successful SEO strategy. Each focuses on different aspects of optimization but works together to improve your site's overall ranking.

1. **On-Page SEO Techniques:**

On-page SEO refers to the practices you can control directly on your website to improve its search engine ranking. Key on-page SEO techniques include:

- **Title Tags:** The title tag is one of the most critical on-page SEO elements. It appears in the SERPs as the clickable headline for your page and should include your primary keyword. Title tags should be concise, descriptive, and no longer than 60 characters.
- **Meta Descriptions:** The meta description is a brief summary of your page's content that appears below the title tag in the SERPs. While it doesn't directly affect rankings, a well-written meta description can improve your click-through rate (CTR). Include your primary keyword and a compelling call to action.
- **Headings (H1, H2, H3):** Use headings to structure your content and make it easier for readers and search engines to understand.

The H1 tag should include your primary keyword and describe the main topic of the page. Use H2 and H3 tags for subheadings that break down the content into smaller, organized sections.

- **Keyword Optimization:** Strategically place your primary keyword and related keywords throughout your content. However, avoid keyword stuffing, which can negatively impact readability and SEO. Aim for a natural keyword density and use synonyms or related terms.
- **Internal Linking:** Internal links connect one page of your website to another, helping search engines crawl your site more effectively. They also keep visitors on your site longer by guiding them to additional relevant content. Use descriptive anchor text that includes keywords where appropriate.
- **Image Optimization:**

Optimize images by compressing them for faster load times and using descriptive file names and alt text. Alt text should describe the image and include relevant keywords, which helps with SEO and accessibility.

- **URL Structure:** Use clean, descriptive URLs that include your primary keyword and reflect the content of the page. Avoid using long strings of numbers or special characters in your URLs.

2. **Off-Page SEO Techniques:** Off-page SEO involves activities outside of your website that influence your search engine rankings. The most important off-page SEO technique is building backlinks, which are links from other websites to your own. Here are some key off-page SEO techniques:
    - **Backlink Building:** Backlinks from reputable, high-authority sites are a strong signal to search engines that your content is valuable.

Focus on earning backlinks through guest blogging, influencer outreach, and creating shareable content. Avoid low-quality backlinks, as they can harm your SEO.

- **Social Media Marketing:** Social signals, such as likes, shares, and comments on social media platforms, can indirectly affect your SEO. While social media activity doesn't directly impact rankings, it can drive traffic to your site and increase the likelihood of earning backlinks.
- **Guest Blogging:** Writing guest posts for reputable blogs in your niche can help you build authority, reach a new audience, and earn backlinks. Make sure to provide high-quality, original content that adds value to the host blog's audience.
- **Online Directories and Citations:**

Submitting your blog to relevant online directories and ensuring your business information is consistent across the web can improve your local SEO and overall online presence.

- **Influencer Marketing:** Collaborating with influencers in your niche can help you gain visibility and credibility. Influencers can link to your content, share it with their followers, and help you build your brand's authority.

Keyword Research and Content Optimization

Keyword research is the foundation of effective SEO. It involves identifying the terms and phrases your target audience is searching for and optimizing your content around those keywords. Here's how to conduct keyword research and optimize your content for better rankings.

1. **The Importance of Keyword Research:**

Keywords are the bridge between what people are searching for and the content you're providing. By targeting the right keywords, you can attract the right audience to your blog and increase your chances of ranking high in the SERPs. Keyword research helps you understand the language your audience uses and the intent behind their searches.

2. **How to Conduct Keyword Research:** There are several tools and techniques you can use to conduct keyword research:
    - **Brainstorm Seed Keywords:** Start by brainstorming a list of seed keywords related to your niche. These are broad terms that represent the main topics of your blog.
    - **Use Keyword Research Tools:** Tools like Google Keyword Planner, Ahrefs, SEMrush, and Ubersuggest can help you find relevant keywords, analyze search volume, and assess keyword difficulty. Look for keywords with high search volume and low competition.
    -

- **Analyze Competitors:** Research your competitors' blogs to identify the keywords they're ranking for. This can give you insights into the keywords that are driving traffic in your niche and help you find opportunities to target similar or related keywords.
- **Consider Long-Tail Keywords:** Long-tail keywords are longer, more specific phrases that often have lower search volume but higher intent. They can be easier to rank for and can drive highly targeted traffic to your blog.
- **Evaluate Keyword Intent:** Understand the intent behind the keywords you're targeting. Are users looking for information, a solution to a problem, or are they ready to make a purchase? Tailor your content to match the intent of the keywords you're targeting.

3. **Content Optimization:** Once you've identified your target keywords, it's time to optimize your content. Here's how:

- **Include Keywords in Strategic Places:** Incorporate your primary keyword in the title tag, meta description, URL, H1 tag, and throughout the content. Also, include related keywords and variations naturally within the text.
- **Write Compelling Meta Descriptions:** Although meta descriptions don't directly impact rankings, they can influence CTR. Write a compelling meta description that includes your primary keyword and entices users to click on your link.
- **Use Structured Data:** Structured data (or schema markup) helps search engines understand the content of your pages better. It can enhance your SERP listing with rich snippets, which can increase CTR.
- **Optimize for Mobile:** Ensure your content is mobile-friendly, as search engines prioritize mobile-optimized sites in their rankings.

This includes using a responsive design, optimizing images, and ensuring fast load times.

- **Monitor and Update Content:** SEO is not a one-time task; it requires ongoing monitoring and updates. Regularly check your rankings, analyze your traffic, and update your content to keep it relevant and optimized.

By mastering SEO, you can significantly increase your blog's visibility, drive more organic traffic, and establish yourself as a leader in your niche. In the next chapter, we'll explore the art of driving traffic to your blog through various channels and turning visitors into loyal readers and customers.

Chapter 8: Building Traffic

Building traffic to your blog is a critical step in growing your online empire. Traffic is the lifeblood of your blog; without it, even the most well-crafted content will go unnoticed. In this chapter, we'll explore strategies to drive traffic to your blog, focusing on leveraging social media, paid advertising, and collaborations such as guest blogging.

Leveraging Social Media for Traffic

Social media platforms are powerful tools for driving traffic to your blog. With billions of active users, social media provides an unparalleled opportunity to reach a broad and engaged audience. Here's how to effectively leverage social media to build traffic:

1. **Choose the Right Platforms:** Not all social media platforms will be suitable for your blog. Focus on the platforms where your target audience is most active.

For example, Instagram and Pinterest are great for visually-driven content, while LinkedIn and Twitter might be more suitable for professional or text-based content.

2. **Create Shareable Content:** The more your content is shared, the more traffic you can drive to your blog. Create content that resonates with your audience, whether it's through stunning visuals, insightful articles, or entertaining videos. Encourage sharing by including social sharing buttons on your blog and by creating content that sparks conversation.
3. **Engage with Your Audience:** Social media is a two-way street. Engage with your audience by responding to comments, participating in discussions, and sharing content that your followers find valuable. Building a community around your brand can lead to more organic shares and increased traffic to your blog.
4. **Utilize Hashtags and Keywords:**

Hashtags on platforms like Instagram, Twitter, and LinkedIn can increase the visibility of your posts to a broader audience. Research and use relevant hashtags that your target audience is following. Similarly, use keywords in your posts and profiles to improve discoverability.

5. **Promote Blog Posts:** Share your blog posts across your social media channels regularly. Create a variety of posts that highlight different aspects of your content to keep your audience engaged. Use eye-catching visuals, compelling headlines, and clear calls-to-action to drive clicks to your blog.
6. **Leverage Influencers:** Collaborate with influencers in your niche to expand your reach. Influencers can share your content with their followers, giving you access to a larger audience. This can be particularly effective if the influencer's audience aligns closely with your target market.

7. **Analyze and Adjust:** Regularly analyze your social media performance using analytics tools provided by each platform. Track metrics such as engagement, click-through rates, and traffic to your blog. Use this data to refine your strategy, focusing on the tactics that are driving the most traffic.

Paid Advertising Strategies

While organic traffic is essential, paid advertising can accelerate your growth by putting your content in front of a larger audience quickly. Here are some effective paid advertising strategies to consider:

1. **Pay-Per-Click (PPC) Advertising:** PPC advertising, such as Google Ads, allows you to place your blog at the top of search engine results for specific keywords. You only pay when someone clicks on your ad, making it a cost-effective way to drive targeted traffic to your blog. Focus on high-intent keywords that are relevant to your content and audience.

2. **Social Media Ads:** Social media platforms like Facebook, Instagram, Twitter, and LinkedIn offer robust advertising options that allow you to target specific demographics, interests, and behaviors. You can use these platforms to promote your blog posts, drive traffic to your website, and even build your email list.
3. **Display Ads:** Display ads are visual advertisements that appear on websites across the internet. These can be effective for retargeting, where you show ads to people who have already visited your blog but didn't take a specific action, such as subscribing or making a purchase. Retargeting helps keep your blog top-of-mind and encourages return visits.
4. **Native Advertising:** Native ads blend seamlessly with the content on the platform where they appear, making them less intrusive and more engaging. Platforms like Outbrain and Taboola offer native advertising opportunities that can drive traffic to your blog by promoting your content on other high-traffic websites.

5. **Sponsored Content:**
Sponsored content involves paying for your blog posts or articles to be featured on other blogs, websites, or social media pages. This can be particularly effective if the content is placed on a site with a large and relevant audience.
6. **Affiliate Marketing Partnerships:**
Partner with other bloggers or influencers who can promote your content through their channels in exchange for a commission on sales or leads generated. This can extend your reach and drive targeted traffic to your blog.
7. **Budgeting and ROI:**
Paid advertising requires careful budgeting to ensure that you're getting a return on your investment (ROI). Set clear goals for your campaigns, whether it's driving traffic, generating leads, or increasing sales. Monitor your ad performance closely and adjust your strategy as needed to maximize your ROI.

Collaborations and Guest Blogging

Collaborations and guest blogging are powerful strategies for building traffic, as they allow you to tap into other bloggers' or influencers' audiences. Here's how to leverage these tactics effectively:

1. **Guest Blogging:** Writing guest posts for other blogs in your niche is one of the best ways to gain exposure and drive traffic to your own blog. Look for high-authority blogs that attract your target audience and pitch them unique, valuable content that aligns with their readers' interests. Include a link back to your blog in your author bio or within the content itself to drive traffic.
2. **Invite Guest Bloggers:** Hosting guest bloggers on your site can also help you attract new readers. When guest bloggers share their posts with their audience, it introduces your blog to a new group of potential readers.

Choose guest bloggers who have a strong following and who can provide high-quality content that resonates with your audience.

3. **Collaborative Content:** Partner with other bloggers or influencers to create collaborative content, such as co-authored articles, joint webinars, or round-up posts. Collaborative content can introduce your blog to a broader audience and provide valuable insights to your readers.
4. **Interviews and Features:** Feature interviews with industry experts, influencers, or successful bloggers in your niche. This not only provides valuable content for your readers but also encourages the featured individuals to share the interview with their audience, driving traffic to your blog.
5. **Content Swaps:** Engage in content swaps with other bloggers, where you exchange blog posts or articles to be featured on each other's sites.

This mutually beneficial arrangement can help both parties increase their reach and traffic.

6. **Cross-Promotions:**
Collaborate with other bloggers or businesses to cross-promote each other's content or products. This can be done through email newsletters, social media shout-outs, or joint contests and giveaways. Cross-promotions are an effective way to reach a new audience and build traffic to your blog.

7. **Link Building:**
Focus on building high-quality backlinks through collaborations and guest blogging. Backlinks not only drive referral traffic but also improve your blog's SEO, making it more likely to rank higher in search engine results.

Building traffic is an ongoing process that requires a combination of organic and paid strategies, as well as collaboration with others in your niche.

By leveraging social media, paid advertising, and collaborations, you can drive a steady stream of traffic to your blog and grow your online empire. In the next chapter, we'll discuss how to turn this traffic into revenue through effective monetization strategies.

Chapter 9: Affiliate Marketing 101

Affiliate marketing is one of the most effective and popular ways to monetize your blog. By promoting products or services and earning a commission on sales or leads generated through your affiliate links, you can create a steady stream of passive income. In this chapter, we'll explore the fundamentals of affiliate marketing, including how to find and join affiliate programs, choosing the right products to promote, and best practices for using affiliate links and disclosures.

How to Find and Join Affiliate Programs

Finding and joining affiliate programs is the first step in building a successful affiliate marketing strategy. Here's how to get started:

1. **Understanding Affiliate Networks vs. Direct Affiliate Programs:** Affiliate programs can be managed through networks or directly by companies.

Affiliate networks are platforms that connect publishers (like bloggers) with a variety of affiliate programs. Popular networks include Amazon Associates, ShareASale, and Commission Junction (CJ). **Direct affiliate programs** are managed by companies themselves, without a third-party network. For example, many SaaS (Software as a Service) companies run their own affiliate programs.

2. **Identifying Relevant Affiliate Programs:** The key to success in affiliate marketing is promoting products or services that are relevant to your audience and align with your niche. Start by researching companies and products that you already use and trust. Then, check if they have an affiliate program. Use affiliate networks to search for programs related to your blog's content.
3. **Joining Affiliate Networks:** To join an affiliate network, you'll typically need to sign up and create a profile.

Some networks require an approval process, where they review your blog to ensure it meets their criteria. Once approved, you'll gain access to a wide range of affiliate programs that you can apply to join.

4. **Applying to Direct Affiliate Programs:** For direct affiliate programs, visit the company's website and look for a link to their affiliate or partner program. The application process usually involves filling out a form with information about your blog, audience, and promotional strategies. Approval times vary, but many programs approve applications within a few days.
5. **Considerations for Choosing Programs:** When evaluating affiliate programs, consider the following factors:
    - **Commission Rates:** Look for programs that offer competitive commission rates. While some programs offer a percentage of the sale, others might pay a flat fee per lead or action.

- **Cookie Duration:** The cookie duration determines how long a user's activity is tracked after they click your affiliate link. Longer cookie durations increase the likelihood of earning commissions.
- **Payout Threshold:** Some programs have minimum payout thresholds that you must reach before you can receive your earnings. Ensure that the threshold aligns with your income goals.
- **Payment Methods:** Check the available payment methods (e.g., PayPal, bank transfer) and ensure they are convenient for you.

6. **Tracking and Managing Affiliate Programs:**

As you join multiple affiliate programs, it's essential to stay organized. Use a spreadsheet or affiliate management tool to track program details, such as login information, commission rates, and payment schedules. This will help you manage your affiliate relationships more effectively.

Choosing the Right Products to Promote

Selecting the right products or services to promote is crucial to your success in affiliate marketing. Here's how to choose wisely:

1. **Relevance to Your Audience:** The products you promote should resonate with your audience's interests, needs, and pain points. Consider the topics you cover on your blog and the types of products that would naturally complement your content. For example, a food blogger might promote kitchen gadgets, cookbooks, or meal delivery services.
2. **Quality and Trustworthiness:** Only promote products that you believe in and that meet high standards of quality. Your audience trusts your recommendations, and promoting subpar products can damage your credibility. Whenever possible, try the products yourself before promoting them.
3. **Profitability:**

While it's important to choose products that align with your niche, you should also consider the potential profitability. Higher-priced products or those with recurring payments (e.g., subscription services) can yield higher commissions. However, balance profitability with relevance and trustworthiness.

4. **Product Demand and Competition:** Research the demand for the products you're considering promoting. High-demand products with low competition can be lucrative opportunities. Use keyword research tools to gauge the popularity of products and assess the competition.
5. **Exclusive Offers and Promotions:** Some affiliate programs offer exclusive deals, discounts, or bonuses that you can pass on to your audience. These offers can make your promotions more appealing and increase conversion rates. Additionally, exclusive offers can help you stand out from other affiliates promoting the same products.

6. **Long-Term Value:** Consider the long-term value of the products you promote. Evergreen products that remain relevant over time can continue to generate commissions long after you've published your content. Additionally, products with upsell opportunities or recurring revenue models can provide ongoing income.

Best Practices for Affiliate Links and Disclosures

Using affiliate links effectively and ethically is key to building a sustainable affiliate marketing business. Here are best practices to follow:

1. **Incorporating Affiliate Links Naturally:** Integrate affiliate links naturally within your content, so they enhance rather than disrupt the reader's experience. For example, include links in product reviews, tutorials, or recommendations that genuinely add value to your readers. Avoid overloading your content with affiliate links, as this can come across as spammy and reduce trust.

2. **Using Clear and Compelling Calls-to-Action:**
Encourage readers to click on your affiliate links by using clear and compelling calls-to-action (CTAs). Phrases like "Check out this amazing product," "Learn more about this service," or "Get a special discount here" can prompt action. Be honest and transparent about what readers can expect when they click the link.
3. **Disclosing Affiliate Relationships:** Transparency is critical in affiliate marketing. It's not only ethical but also legally required to disclose your affiliate relationships. Place a clear disclosure at the beginning of your blog posts, within the content, or near affiliate links. Use straightforward language, such as "This post contains affiliate links. If you click on a link and make a purchase, I may earn a commission at no extra cost to you."
4. **Using Affiliate Disclosures Consistently:**

Ensure that you consistently include disclosures on all pages where affiliate links are present, including blog posts, emails, and social media posts. For social media, use hashtags like #ad, #affiliate, or #sponsored to comply with platform guidelines.

5. **Tracking Link Performance:** Monitor the performance of your affiliate links to understand which products and placements generate the most clicks and conversions. Most affiliate programs provide tracking tools, but you can also use link shorteners or UTM parameters to gather data. Analyzing this data helps you refine your strategy and focus on the most profitable opportunities.
6. **Avoiding Common Pitfalls:** Be cautious of common affiliate marketing mistakes, such as promoting too many products at once, relying on a single source of affiliate income, or failing to provide adequate value in your content.

7. Instead, focus on building trust with your audience by providing genuine recommendations and maintaining a balanced approach to monetization.

Affiliate marketing can be a powerful revenue stream when done correctly. By finding the right programs, choosing relevant products, and following best practices for link usage and disclosures, you can build a sustainable and profitable affiliate marketing business. In the next chapter, we'll dive into additional monetization strategies that can complement your affiliate marketing efforts, helping you maximize the revenue potential of your blog.

Chapter 10: Monetizing Through Blogging

Monetizing your blog effectively requires a multifaceted approach that goes beyond affiliate marketing. By diversifying your income streams, you can create a stable and lucrative business that isn't reliant on a single source of revenue. In this chapter, we'll explore various strategies for monetizing your blog, including sponsored posts, ads, and other revenue sources, as well as creating and selling your own products.

Diversifying Income Streams

Diversifying your income streams is essential for building a sustainable and resilient blogging business. Relying on a single source of income, such as affiliate marketing, can leave you vulnerable to changes in the market or fluctuations in your earnings. Here's how to diversify your blog's income:

1. **Affiliate Marketing:**
As discussed in the previous chapter, affiliate marketing is a powerful way to generate income by promoting products or services that align with your niche. However, it should be just one part of your overall monetization strategy.
2. **Display Advertising:**
Display ads are a common and straightforward way to monetize your blog. By partnering with ad networks like Google AdSense or Media.net, you can earn money every time a visitor views or clicks on an ad placed on your blog. While display ads might not generate substantial income on their own, they can provide a steady stream of revenue, especially as your traffic grows.
3. **Sponsored Content:**
Sponsored posts and content partnerships are another lucrative income stream. Brands pay you to create content that promotes their products or services. Sponsored content can take many forms, including blog posts, social media posts, videos, or product reviews.

To attract sponsorships, focus on building a strong online presence and engaging with your audience.

4. **Product Sales:**
Selling your own products is one of the most profitable ways to monetize your blog. Whether you offer digital products like eBooks, courses, and printables, or physical products like merchandise and handmade items, creating and selling your own products allows you to retain full control over your revenue. We'll explore this in more detail later in the chapter.
5. **Memberships and Subscriptions:** Membership or subscription models allow you to generate recurring revenue by offering exclusive content, resources, or services to your most loyal readers. Platforms like Patreon, Substack, or your own website can be used to manage memberships and subscriptions. This model works well if you have a dedicated following that values premium content or experiences.
6. **Freelance Services:**

If you have expertise in writing, graphic design, web development, or another skill related to your blog's niche, offering freelance services can be an additional income stream. Use your blog to showcase your portfolio and attract clients who need your services. Freelance work can provide a significant boost to your income, especially if you're just starting.

7. **Consulting and Coaching:** As your blog grows and you establish yourself as an authority in your niche, you can offer consulting or coaching services. Whether it's one-on-one sessions, group coaching, or consulting for businesses, these services can be highly profitable. They also position you as a thought leader and build deeper relationships with your audience.

Sponsored Posts, Ads, and Other Revenue Sources

In addition to diversifying your income streams, let's dive deeper into specific strategies like sponsored posts, ads, and other revenue sources:

1. **Sponsored Posts:**
Sponsored posts involve creating content on behalf of a brand in exchange for payment. These posts can be product reviews, tutorials, or general articles that align with the brand's goals. To succeed with sponsored posts, follow these tips:
    - **Be Selective:** Only work with brands that align with your values and are relevant to your audience. Promoting products that don't resonate with your readers can damage your credibility.
    - **Disclose Sponsored Content:** Transparency is crucial. Clearly disclose when a post is sponsored, as required by legal regulations and to maintain trust with your audience.
    - **Negotiate Fair Compensation:** Ensure that you're compensated fairly for your time and effort. Consider factors like the scope of work, audience size, and potential reach when setting your rates.
2. **Display Ads:**

Display ads are a passive way to earn income as your blog traffic grows. Here's how to maximize your ad revenue:

- **Choose the Right Ad Network:** Start with beginner-friendly networks like Google AdSense, but consider transitioning to premium ad networks like Mediavine or AdThrive as your traffic increases.
- **Optimize Ad Placement:** Experiment with ad placement to find the spots that generate the most clicks without disrupting the user experience. Common ad placements include the header, sidebar, and within content.
- **Monitor Performance:** Regularly review your ad performance to identify opportunities for optimization. Factors like ad size, format, and placement can impact earnings.

3. **Selling Ad Space Directly:** As your blog grows, you may attract brands interested in buying ad space directly from you.

Selling ad space directly allows you to negotiate higher rates than what ad networks typically offer. It also gives you more control over the types of ads displayed on your site. Here's how to do it:

- **Create a Media Kit:** A media kit is a document that outlines your blog's key metrics, audience demographics, and advertising options. It's an essential tool for pitching to potential advertisers.
- **Set Your Rates:** Determine your rates based on factors like your blog's traffic, niche, and audience engagement. Be prepared to negotiate with advertisers to find a mutually beneficial arrangement.
- **Build Relationships:** Foster long-term relationships with advertisers by delivering results and maintaining open communication. Satisfied advertisers are more likely to renew their contracts or refer you to others.

4. **Affiliate Ads:**

In addition to regular display ads, consider incorporating affiliate ads into your blog. These are ads for products or services you're an affiliate for, and you earn a commission on any sales generated through clicks on these ads. Affiliate ads can be more profitable than regular display ads because they offer the potential for higher commissions.

5. **Email Marketing for Monetization:** Building an email list is one of the most valuable assets for a blogger. Your email subscribers are a captive audience who are more likely to engage with your content and promotions. Here's how to monetize through email marketing:
    - **Promote Affiliate Products:** Include affiliate product recommendations in your email newsletters. Personalize your recommendations based on your subscribers' interests and previous engagement.
    - **Offer Exclusive Deals:**

Negotiate exclusive discounts or offers with brands and share them with your email list. This adds value to your subscribers while generating income for you.

- **Launch Your Products:** When launching your own products, your email list will be one of the most effective channels for driving sales. Build anticipation and offer early access or special discounts to your subscribers.

6. **Monetizing Videos and Webinars:** If your blog includes video content or you host webinars, there are several ways to monetize these formats:
    - **YouTube Ads:** If you have a YouTube channel, you can monetize it through ads by joining the YouTube Partner Program. As your channel grows, you can also explore sponsorships and brand deals.
    - **Webinar Sponsorships:**

Partner with brands to sponsor your webinars. In exchange for their sponsorship, you can promote their products during the webinar or offer attendees exclusive discounts.

- **Video Courses:** If you have expertise in a particular area, consider creating video courses and selling them through your blog. Platforms like Teachable, Udemy, or your own website can help you deliver and monetize your courses.

Creating and Selling Your Own Products

One of the most effective ways to monetize your blog and gain full control over your income is by creating and selling your own products. Here's how to turn your expertise into profitable products:

1. **Digital Products:** Digital products are popular because they require minimal overhead and can be sold repeatedly. Here are some ideas for digital products:

- **eBooks:** Write an eBook on a topic that resonates with your audience. eBooks are relatively easy to create and can be sold on your blog or through platforms like Amazon Kindle.
- **Online Courses:** Create comprehensive online courses that teach your audience valuable skills. Platforms like Teachable, Kajabi, or Thinkific make it easy to create and sell courses.
- **Printables:** Design printables such as planners, checklists, or worksheets that your audience can download and use. Printables are often low-cost and can be a great way to generate passive income.
- **Membership Sites:** Offer premium content, resources, or community access through a membership site. Charge a monthly or annual fee for access, creating a recurring revenue stream.

2. Physical Products:

If you have the means to manage inventory, selling physical products can be a lucrative option. Here are some examples:

- **Merchandise:** Create branded merchandise such as T-shirts, mugs, or tote bags that reflect your blog's identity. Use print-on-demand services like Printful or Teespring to handle production and shipping.
- **Handmade Goods:** If you have a talent for crafting, consider selling handmade goods like jewelry, artwork, or home decor. Use your blog to showcase your products and drive sales.
- **Books:** If you've written a book, consider self-publishing and selling it directly through your blog. Physical books can be sold alongside digital versions to cater to different customer preferences.

3. **Services and Consulting:**

Offering services or consulting is a natural extension of your blog's content. Whether you're providing one-on-one coaching, group workshops, or custom services, here's how to monetize your expertise:

- **Coaching Programs:** Develop structured coaching programs that guide clients through a specific transformation. This could be anything from business coaching to personal development or health and wellness coaching.
- **Consulting Services:** Offer consulting services to businesses or individuals who need specialized advice. Use your blog to demonstrate your expertise and attract high-paying clients.
- **Freelance Services:** If you have a skill like writing, design, or marketing, offer freelance services to your audience. Position yourself as an expert in your niche, and use your blog as a portfolio to showcase your work.

4. **Building an Online Store:** If you're selling physical or digital products, consider setting up an online store on your blog. Platforms like WooCommerce (for WordPress) or Shopify make it easy to create a professional store. Here's how to get started:
    - **Choose a Platform:** Select an eCommerce platform that integrates seamlessly with your blog. WooCommerce is a popular choice for WordPress users, while Shopify is a standalone platform that's user-friendly and robust.
    - **Set Up Your Store:** Design your online store with user experience in mind. Ensure that it's easy for visitors to browse products, add items to their cart, and complete the checkout process.
    - **Optimize for Conversions:** Use persuasive product descriptions, high-quality images, and clear calls-to-action to encourage visitors to make a purchase.

Implement trust signals, such as customer reviews and secure payment options, to build confidence.

Monetizing your blog through various channels not only increases your revenue potential but also provides financial stability by diversifying your income streams. Whether you're earning from sponsored posts, ads, affiliate marketing, or your own products, the key to success lies in understanding your audience and offering value at every turn. As you continue to build your blog and explore different monetization strategies, remember that persistence, creativity, and a deep connection with your audience are the foundation of a thriving blogging business.

Chapter 11: Maximizing Conversion Rates

Maximizing your blog's conversion rates is essential for turning traffic into tangible results. Whether your goal is to increase sales, generate leads, or grow your email list, optimizing conversion rates will ensure that your efforts yield the best possible outcomes. In this chapter, we'll explore how to craft compelling calls-to-action, leverage email marketing for conversions, and use analytics to refine your strategies.

Crafting Compelling Calls-to-Action

A call-to-action (CTA) is a prompt that encourages your audience to take a specific action, such as signing up for your newsletter, purchasing a product, or sharing a post. The effectiveness of your CTAs directly impacts your conversion rates, making it crucial to craft them thoughtfully.

1. **Be Clear and Direct:**

Your CTA should be straightforward and easy to understand. Avoid vague language and ensure that your audience knows exactly what they'll get by taking the action you're promoting. For example, instead of saying, "Click here," use "Download your free eBook now" or "Join our community today."

2. **Use Action-Oriented Language:** Powerful verbs like "Get," "Download," "Start," or "Discover" can inspire action. These words create a sense of urgency and excitement, making it more likely that your audience will respond. Pair these verbs with benefit-driven language to emphasize the value of taking action.
3. **Make It Visually Appealing:** Design your CTA buttons or links to stand out on the page. Use contrasting colors that draw the eye and make the CTA visually distinct from the rest of your content. Ensure the text is easy to read and the button size is large enough to be clickable on both desktop and mobile devices.

4. **Create a Sense of Urgency:** Incorporating urgency into your CTAs can prompt immediate action. Phrases like "Limited Time Offer," "Only a Few Spots Left," or "Sign Up Before Midnight" create a fear of missing out (FOMO), encouraging your audience to act quickly.
5. **Test and Optimize:** A/B testing different CTAs can help you identify which ones perform best. Test variations in wording, color, placement, and size to see which combinations drive the highest conversions. Use the results to continuously refine your CTAs for maximum impact.
6. **Positioning Matters:** Place your CTAs in prominent positions where they're most likely to be seen and clicked. Common placements include above the fold, at the end of blog posts, within the content, and in sidebars. Consider using multiple CTAs throughout your content to capture attention at different points.

Email Marketing for Conversions

Email marketing is one of the most effective tools for converting prospects into customers. With a well-crafted email strategy, you can nurture your audience, build relationships, and drive conversions. Here's how to use email marketing to boost your conversion rates:

1. **Segment Your Audience:** Segmenting your email list allows you to send targeted messages that resonate with specific groups within your audience. Segmentation can be based on factors like demographics, purchase history, behavior, or engagement level. By delivering relevant content to each segment, you increase the likelihood of conversions.
2. **Personalize Your Emails:** Personalization goes beyond using the recipient's name in the email greeting. Tailor your content to address the specific needs, interests, and pain points of your audience.

For example, if you're promoting a product, highlight how it solves a particular problem that your recipient is facing.

3. **Craft Compelling Subject Lines:** Your subject line is the first thing your audience sees, so it needs to grab their attention. A compelling subject line should be concise, intriguing, and relevant to the content of the email. Consider using personalization, curiosity, or urgency to encourage opens.
4. **Focus on Value:** Every email you send should offer value to your subscribers. Whether it's useful information, a special offer, or exclusive content, ensure that your emails are worth opening. When your audience perceives value, they're more likely to engage with your content and take action.
5. **Include Strong CTAs:** Just like on your blog, your emails should include clear and compelling CTAs.

Whether you want your audience to make a purchase, sign up for a webinar, or download a resource, make the desired action obvious and easy to complete. Place your CTA prominently within the email and consider including it more than once.

6. **Automate Your Email Campaigns:** Automation allows you to send timely and relevant emails based on your audience's behavior or specific triggers. For example, you can set up a welcome series for new subscribers, abandoned cart reminders for shoppers, or follow-up emails after a purchase. Automated emails help maintain engagement and drive conversions without manual effort.

7. **Analyze and Optimize:** Regularly review the performance of your email campaigns to identify areas for improvement. Track metrics like open rates, click-through rates, conversion rates, and unsubscribe rates. Use this data to optimize your subject lines, content, CTAs, and timing for better results.

Using Analytics to Refine Your Strategies

Analytics provide valuable insights into how your audience interacts with your content, helping you make data-driven decisions to improve your conversion rates. By understanding what works and what doesn't, you can refine your strategies for better results.

1. **Track Key Metrics:** Identify the key performance indicators (KPIs) that matter most for your conversion goals. Common metrics include:
    - **Conversion Rate:** The percentage of visitors who complete the desired action, such as making a purchase or signing up for a newsletter.
    - **Bounce Rate:** The percentage of visitors who leave your site after viewing only one page. A high bounce rate may indicate that your content or user experience needs improvement.
    - **Click-Through Rate (CTR):** The percentage of people who click on a CTA or link within your content.

CTR is a strong indicator of how compelling your CTAs are.

- **Average Time on Page:** The amount of time visitors spend on a page. Longer times may indicate that your content is engaging and informative.
- **Customer Lifetime Value (CLV):** The total revenue generated by a customer over the entire duration of their relationship with your brand.

2. **Use Analytics Tools:** Leverage tools like Google Analytics, heatmaps, and A/B testing platforms to gain deeper insights into user behavior. Google Analytics provides detailed data on traffic sources, user demographics, and behavior flow, while heatmaps show where users click and scroll on your pages. A/B testing tools help you compare different versions of a page or CTA to see which one performs better.
3. **Identify Patterns and Trends:** Look for patterns and trends in your analytics data that can inform your strategy.

For example, if you notice that a particular blog post is driving a lot of traffic but has a low conversion rate, you might need to optimize the CTAs or update the content to better align with your audience's needs.

4. **Test and Iterate:** Continuous testing and iteration are key to improving conversion rates. Experiment with different elements of your content, such as headlines, images, CTAs, and layout, to see what resonates best with your audience. Use A/B testing to validate your changes and make data-backed decisions.
5. **Optimize for Mobile:** With an increasing number of users accessing content on mobile devices, it's crucial to ensure that your blog and emails are mobile-friendly. Use responsive design, simplify navigation, and optimize load times to provide a seamless experience for mobile users. Mobile optimization can significantly impact conversion rates, as a poor mobile experience can lead to higher bounce rates.

6. **Refine Your Audience Targeting:** Use analytics to understand your audience's behavior and preferences better. Refine your targeting strategies based on the insights you gather, focusing on reaching the right people with the right message at the right time. Consider factors like geographic location, device usage, and user intent when tailoring your content and CTAs.

By crafting compelling CTAs, leveraging email marketing effectively, and using analytics to refine your strategies, you can significantly boost your conversion rates. Remember, the key to success lies in continuous optimization and a deep understanding of your audience. As you fine-tune your approach, you'll be better equipped to turn your blog's traffic into meaningful and profitable actions.

Chapter 12: Scaling and Automating

Scaling and Automating

Building a successful blog and affiliate marketing business is just the beginning. To truly dominate the digital space, you need to think about scaling your operations and automating key processes. Scaling allows you to expand your reach, increase your revenue, and solidify your brand's presence. Automation, on the other hand, frees up your time, allowing you to focus on growth and strategic decision-making. This chapter will guide you through the process of scaling your online business, including expanding your content and reach, building a team, and leveraging automation tools.

Scaling Your Online Business

As your blog and affiliate marketing efforts start to gain traction, it's essential to think about how you can scale your operations.

Scaling involves growing your business in a sustainable way, ensuring that you can handle increased traffic, sales, and customer demands without compromising quality or efficiency.

Expanding Your Content and Reach

1. **Diversify Your Content Offerings:** As you scale, consider expanding the types of content you produce. While blog posts may be your primary content, you can reach new audiences and enhance engagement by diversifying your content offerings. This might include:
    - **Video Content:** Create video tutorials, product reviews, or behind-the-scenes content to engage with your audience in a more dynamic way. Platforms like YouTube and TikTok can help you reach a wider audience and drive traffic back to your blog.
    - **Podcasts:** Launch a podcast where you discuss industry trends, interview experts, or share personal insights.

Podcasts are an excellent way to build a deeper connection with your audience and establish your authority in your niche.

- **Webinars and Live Streams:** Host live events where you can interact with your audience in real-time. Webinars and live streams are particularly effective for selling products, conducting Q&A sessions, and offering value-packed presentations.

2. **Expand Your Audience:** Scaling your business also means reaching new audiences. This can be achieved through various strategies:
    - **Internationalization:** If your content is primarily in one language, consider translating it into other languages to reach non-English-speaking markets. This could involve creating multilingual versions of your blog or hiring translators.
    - **Content Repurposing:**

Repurpose existing content into different formats to appeal to different segments of your audience. For example, turn a blog post into an infographic, a video, or a podcast episode. This not only saves time but also maximizes the value of your content.

- **Guest Posting:** Collaborate with other bloggers and influencers by writing guest posts for their blogs or having them contribute to yours. Guest posting helps you tap into their audience and build backlinks, which can boost your SEO and drive traffic.

3. **Increase Your Publishing Frequency:** As you grow, consider increasing the frequency of your content publication. More content means more opportunities to attract traffic, engage with your audience, and generate revenue. However, it's important to maintain quality even as you scale quantity.

If managing a higher publishing frequency is challenging, consider outsourcing content creation.

4. **Explore New Channels:** Don't limit yourself to just one or two platforms. As you scale, explore additional channels to promote your content and affiliate offers. This could include:
    - **Social Media Expansion:** If you're only active on a couple of social media platforms, consider expanding to others where your target audience might be. For example, if you're currently on Instagram and Facebook, you might explore Pinterest, LinkedIn, or Twitter.
    - **Email Marketing Growth:** Continue to grow your email list by offering new lead magnets and exclusive content. Segment your list to send more targeted emails and consider implementing advanced email automation to nurture leads and drive conversions.
    - **Paid Advertising:**

Invest in paid advertising campaigns to accelerate growth. Platforms like Google Ads, Facebook Ads, and Instagram Ads allow you to reach a larger audience quickly. As you scale, consider increasing your ad spend and experimenting with different ad formats and targeting options.

Building a Team and Outsourcing

As your business grows, managing everything on your own can become overwhelming. Building a team and outsourcing tasks is crucial for scaling efficiently. Delegating responsibilities allows you to focus on high-level strategy and growth while ensuring that day-to-day operations run smoothly.

1. **Identify Key Roles:** Start by identifying the key roles you need to fill. Common roles in a growing online business include:
    - **Content Creators:** Writers, video editors, and graphic designers who can help produce high-quality content.

- **Social Media Managers:** Professionals who can manage your social media presence, engage with your audience, and run paid advertising campaigns.
- **SEO Specialists:** Experts who can optimize your content for search engines, conduct keyword research, and build backlinks.
- **Web Developers:** Developers who can maintain and improve your website's functionality, design, and user experience.
- **Customer Support:** As your audience grows, you may need a dedicated team to handle customer inquiries, feedback, and support requests.

2. **Outsource Non-Core Tasks:** Outsourcing non-core tasks allows you to focus on what you do best while leaving specialized tasks to experts. Consider outsourcing the following:
   - **Content Creation:** Hire freelance writers, designers, and videographers to produce content.

Platforms like Upwork, Fiverr, and Contently are great places to find skilled freelancers.

- **Technical Maintenance:** If you're not tech-savvy, outsource website maintenance, plugin updates, and security monitoring to a professional.
- **Administrative Tasks:** Virtual assistants (VAs) can handle tasks like email management, scheduling, data entry, and customer service.

3. **Build a Remote Team:** A remote team offers flexibility and access to a global talent pool. Use collaboration tools like Slack, Asana, or Trello to manage projects, communicate with team members, and track progress. Ensure that you have clear processes and guidelines in place to maintain consistency and quality across your operations.
4. **Foster a Positive Work Culture:** Even with a remote team, it's essential to foster a positive work culture.

Encourage open communication, recognize and reward contributions, and provide opportunities for professional growth. A motivated and engaged team is more likely to deliver high-quality work and contribute to your business's success.

Leveraging Automation Tools

Automation is key to scaling efficiently. By automating repetitive tasks, you can save time, reduce errors, and focus on strategic growth. Here's how to leverage automation tools to streamline your operations:

1. **Automate Content Distribution:** Use automation tools to schedule and distribute your content across various platforms. Tools like Buffer, Hootsuite, and CoSchedule allow you to plan and automate social media posts, ensuring consistent promotion without manual effort.

You can also automate email newsletters using platforms like Mailchimp or ConvertKit, delivering your content to subscribers at the optimal time.

2. **Email Marketing Automation:** Email automation is essential for nurturing leads and driving conversions. Set up automated email sequences to welcome new subscribers, follow up with leads, and send personalized recommendations. For example:
    - **Welcome Series:** Automatically send a series of emails to new subscribers, introducing them to your brand and offering valuable content.
    - **Abandoned Cart Emails:** For eCommerce businesses, set up automated emails to remind customers who left items in their cart to complete their purchase.
    - **Re-engagement Campaigns:** Automate emails to re-engage inactive subscribers with special offers, updates, or exclusive content.

3. **Sales and Marketing Automation:** Automation tools can help streamline your sales and marketing processes. For example:
    - **CRM Tools:** Customer relationship management (CRM) tools like HubSpot or Salesforce can automate lead tracking, follow-ups, and customer segmentation.
    - **Lead Scoring:** Use lead scoring to prioritize high-potential leads and automate follow-up actions based on lead behavior and engagement.
    - **Affiliate Marketing Automation:** If you're managing multiple affiliate partnerships, use tools like Tapfiliate or Refersion to automate tracking, reporting, and commission payments.
4. **Analytics and Reporting:** Automate your analytics and reporting to gain real-time insights into your business performance. Tools like Google Analytics, SEMrush, and Ahrefs can automatically track metrics like traffic, conversions, and keyword rankings.

Set up automated reports to receive regular updates on your key performance indicators (KPIs), helping you make informed decisions without manual data collection.

5. **Customer Support Automation:**
As your audience grows, automating customer support can help you manage inquiries more efficiently. Implement chatbots on your website to handle common questions and guide visitors through your sales funnel. Use tools like Zendesk or Freshdesk to automate ticketing and support workflows, ensuring timely responses to customer queries.

6. **Task Management and Workflow Automation:**
Automate repetitive tasks and workflows to improve productivity. Tools like Zapier and Integromat allow you to connect different apps and automate actions based on triggers.

For example, you can automatically add new leads from your website to your CRM, schedule tasks based on email receipts, or update your social media calendar when a new blog post is published.

Conclusion

Scaling and automating your online business are crucial steps in achieving digital dominance. By expanding your content and reach, building a strong team, and leveraging automation tools, you can handle increased demands without sacrificing quality or efficiency. Remember that scaling is not just about growing your audience and revenue—it's also about creating sustainable systems that allow your business to thrive in the long term.

As you continue to scale, stay focused on delivering value to your audience, maintaining a strong brand identity, and continuously optimizing your operations. With the right strategies in place, your journey from zero to online empire will not only be achievable but also rewarding and impactful.

Chapter 13: Advanced Affiliate Marketing Techniques

As your affiliate marketing business matures, it's essential to delve into advanced techniques that can elevate your strategy and drive significant growth. This chapter explores leveraging data and analytics for informed decision-making, exploring advanced marketing channels, and creating high-converting funnels. By incorporating these advanced techniques, you'll be well-positioned to scale your efforts and maximize your revenue potential.

Leveraging Data and Analytics for Growth

Data and analytics are invaluable tools for refining your affiliate marketing strategies and achieving sustained growth. By understanding and analyzing your performance metrics, you can make data-driven decisions that enhance your effectiveness and optimize your campaigns.

1. **Track and Analyze Key Metrics:** To leverage data effectively, start by tracking and analyzing key performance indicators (KPIs). These metrics include:
    - **Conversion Rate:** The percentage of visitors who complete the desired action (e.g., making a purchase through your affiliate link). Monitoring this metric helps you gauge the effectiveness of your affiliate offers and content.
    - **Click-Through Rate (CTR):** The ratio of users who click on your affiliate links compared to the total number of users who view them. A high CTR indicates that your content and CTAs are engaging and persuasive.
    - **Cost Per Acquisition (CPA):** The cost associated with acquiring a customer through your affiliate links. Tracking CPA helps you evaluate the efficiency of your campaigns and manage your budget effectively.
    - **Return on Investment (ROI):**

The profitability of your affiliate marketing efforts. Calculating ROI involves comparing the revenue generated from affiliate sales against the costs incurred (e.g., advertising spend, content creation).

2. **Use Analytics Tools:** Utilize analytics tools to gain deeper insights into your affiliate marketing performance. Tools like Google Analytics, affiliate network dashboards, and third-party analytics platforms provide comprehensive data on user behavior, traffic sources, and campaign performance. Key features to explore include:
    - **Conversion Tracking:** Set up conversion tracking to monitor which affiliate links are generating sales and which sources are most effective.
    - **Behavior Analysis:** Analyze user behavior on your site to understand how visitors interact with your content and affiliate links. Look for patterns that indicate which content drives the most conversions.

- **Attribution Modeling:** Use attribution modeling to determine how different marketing channels contribute to conversions. This helps you allocate your resources more effectively and understand the customer journey.
3. **A/B Testing for Optimization:** Conduct A/B testing to optimize your affiliate marketing campaigns. By comparing two variations of a campaign element (e.g., CTA button color, landing page layout), you can determine which version performs better. Implementing the winning variation can lead to improved conversion rates and overall campaign success.
4. **Data-Driven Insights:** Use the insights gained from your data analysis to make informed decisions. For example:
    - **Content Optimization:** If data shows that certain types of content drive higher conversions, focus on creating similar content. Optimize existing content based on performance metrics.

- **Audience Targeting:** Refine your audience targeting based on demographic and behavioral data. Tailor your affiliate offers and marketing messages to better align with your audience's preferences and interests.
- **Campaign Adjustments:** Adjust your marketing strategies and budgets based on performance data. Reallocate resources to the most effective channels and campaigns to maximize ROI.

Exploring Advanced Marketing Channels

Expanding into advanced marketing channels can provide new opportunities to reach and engage your audience. Here are some advanced channels and strategies to consider:

1. **Influencer Marketing:** Collaborate with influencers in your niche to promote affiliate products.

Influencers have established trust with their audience, and their endorsements can drive significant traffic and conversions. Key considerations for influencer marketing include:

- **Identify Relevant Influencers:** Look for influencers whose audience aligns with your target market. Use tools like AspireIQ, Traackr, or Upfluence to find and evaluate potential influencers.
- **Create Authentic Partnerships:** Develop genuine relationships with influencers and ensure that their content aligns with your brand values. Authentic endorsements are more likely to resonate with their audience.
- **Negotiate Terms:** Clearly define the terms of the partnership, including compensation, deliverables, and performance metrics. Establish clear expectations to ensure a successful collaboration.

2. **Affiliate Networks and Platforms:**

Explore opportunities with affiliate networks and platforms that offer advanced features and a wide range of affiliate programs. These networks can provide access to additional resources, tools, and support. Some popular affiliate networks include:

- **CJ Affiliate:** Offers a large network of advertisers and advanced reporting tools for tracking performance.
- **ShareASale:** Provides a diverse selection of merchants and detailed analytics for optimizing your affiliate campaigns.
- **Rakuten Marketing:** Known for its comprehensive tracking capabilities and access to global affiliate programs.

3. **Native Advertising:** Native advertising blends seamlessly with the content on the platform where it appears, making it less intrusive and more engaging. Consider using native ads to promote your affiliate products in a way that complements the user experience. Platforms like Taboola and Outbrain specialize in native advertising.

4. **Video Marketing:**
   Incorporate video content into your affiliate marketing strategy. Videos can be highly engaging and persuasive, making them effective for promoting products. Consider creating product reviews, tutorials, and comparison videos to drive traffic and conversions. Platforms like YouTube and TikTok offer opportunities to reach a broad audience through video.
5. **Podcast Advertising:**
   If you host or sponsor podcasts, leverage them to promote affiliate products. Podcasts have a loyal and engaged audience, and endorsements from podcast hosts can drive conversions. Work with podcast producers or hosts to create sponsored content or ad placements that highlight your affiliate offers.

Creating High-Converting Funnels

A well-designed sales funnel guides potential customers through the buying process, from initial awareness to final purchase.

By creating high-converting funnels, you can optimize each stage of the customer journey and increase your affiliate marketing success.

1. **Understanding the Funnel Stages:** A typical sales funnel consists of the following stages:
    - **Awareness:** Attract potential customers through content, ads, or other marketing efforts. The goal is to introduce them to your brand and affiliate offers.
    - **Interest:** Engage prospects by providing valuable content and addressing their needs or pain points. This stage involves nurturing leads and building relationships.
    - **Decision:** Present compelling offers and incentives that encourage prospects to take action. This might include product reviews, testimonials, or special discounts.
    - **Action:**

Drive conversions by guiding prospects to complete the desired action, such as making a purchase or signing up for a service.

2. **Designing Effective Lead Magnets:** Offer valuable lead magnets to capture contact information and nurture leads. Lead magnets can include:
    - **Ebooks or Guides:** Provide in-depth information or resources related to your niche. Ensure that the content is relevant and valuable to your audience.
    - **Checklists or Templates:** Offer practical tools that help your audience achieve their goals or solve specific problems.
    - **Free Trials or Samples:** Allow potential customers to experience the product or service before making a purchase decision.

3. **Crafting Persuasive Landing Pages:** Design landing pages that are optimized for conversions. Key elements of a high-converting landing page include:

- **Clear Headline:** Use a compelling headline that clearly communicates the value proposition and entices visitors to stay on the page.
- **Engaging Content:** Provide concise and persuasive content that highlights the benefits of the affiliate product or service.
- **Strong CTA:** Include a prominent and action-oriented call-to-action button that encourages visitors to take the next step in the funnel.
- **Social Proof:** Incorporate testimonials, reviews, or case studies to build trust and credibility.

4. **Implementing Retargeting Strategies:** Retargeting involves reaching out to users who have previously interacted with your site but did not convert. Implement retargeting campaigns to remind and re-engage potential customers. Use tools like Google Ads or Facebook Ads to create retargeting ads that offer additional incentives or address any objections.

5. **Optimizing and Testing Funnels:** Continuously optimize your sales funnels by testing different elements and analyzing performance data. Conduct A/B testing on headlines, CTAs, and offers to determine which variations drive the highest conversion rates. Use analytics tools to track funnel performance and identify areas for improvement.
6. **Automating Funnel Processes:** Implement automation tools to streamline and manage your sales funnel processes. For example:
    - **Email Automation:** Set up automated email sequences to nurture leads and guide them through the funnel stages.
    - **CRM Integration:** Use CRM tools to manage and track leads, automate follow-ups, and personalize communication.
    - **Funnel Software:** Consider using funnel-building software like ClickFunnels or Leadpages to create and manage your funnels more efficiently.

Conclusion

Mastering advanced affiliate marketing techniques can significantly enhance your growth and success in the digital space. By leveraging data and analytics, exploring advanced marketing channels, and creating high-converting funnels, you'll be able to optimize your strategies, reach new audiences, and drive higher conversions. Remember, the key to sustained success lies in continuous learning, experimentation, and adaptation. With these advanced techniques in your toolkit, you're well-equipped to take your affiliate marketing efforts to new heights and achieve long-term success.

Chapter 14: Maintaining Your Online Empire

Building an online empire through affiliate marketing and blogging is a significant achievement, but sustaining that success over the long term requires careful planning and consistent effort. This chapter focuses on long-term strategies for maintaining your online empire, staying ahead of industry trends, and avoiding common pitfalls that can derail your progress.

Long-Term Strategies for Sustained Success

1. **Continuous Learning and Adaptation:**
    - **Evolving with the Market:** The digital landscape is constantly changing, with new tools, platforms, and strategies emerging regularly. To maintain your online empire, it's essential to stay informed and adapt to these changes.

Invest time in continuous learning through online courses, industry blogs, webinars, and networking with other professionals in your niche.

- **Embracing Innovation:** Be open to experimenting with new technologies and marketing techniques. Whether it's adopting AI-driven tools for content creation, exploring emerging social media platforms, or using advanced analytics for more precise targeting, innovation can keep your empire at the cutting edge.

2. **Consistent Content Creation:**
    - **Regular Content Updates:** Keep your blog and other content channels fresh by consistently updating old content and creating new, valuable content. Regularly updated content not only keeps your audience engaged but also signals to search engines that your site is active, which can positively impact your rankings.

- **Diversifying Content Formats:** To cater to different audience preferences, diversify your content formats. Incorporate videos, podcasts, infographics, and interactive content alongside traditional blog posts. This variety can attract a broader audience and enhance user engagement.

3. **Building and Nurturing Relationships:**
    - **Engaging with Your Audience:** Your audience is the lifeblood of your online empire. Engage with them through comments, social media, email newsletters, and other communication channels. Responding to their feedback and addressing their needs builds loyalty and trust, ensuring they remain invested in your brand.
    - **Networking with Industry Peers:** Forming alliances and partnerships with other influencers, bloggers, and businesses in your niche can open new opportunities for growth.

Collaborations, guest posts, joint ventures, and affiliate partnerships can all contribute to sustaining your success.

4. **Diversifying Income Streams:**
    - **Expanding Monetization Avenues:** Relying solely on affiliate marketing for income can be risky, especially if the market shifts or affiliate programs change. Diversify your revenue streams by exploring other monetization options like creating and selling digital products, offering consulting services, launching membership sites, or developing online courses.
    - **Reinvesting in Your Business:** Allocate a portion of your earnings to reinvest in your business. This could mean upgrading your website, hiring additional team members, enhancing your marketing efforts, or investing in paid advertising to reach new audiences.

Staying Ahead of Industry Trends

1. **Monitoring Industry Developments:**
   - **Keeping Up with Trends:** Stay informed about the latest trends in digital marketing, affiliate marketing, and blogging. Subscribe to industry newsletters, follow thought leaders on social media, and attend conferences or webinars to gain insights into emerging trends.
   - **Analyzing Competitors:** Regularly monitor your competitors to see what strategies they are implementing. Analyzing their content, marketing tactics, and audience engagement can provide inspiration and help you identify opportunities for differentiation.
2. **Adopting Emerging Technologies:**
   - **Exploring AI and Automation:** As artificial intelligence and automation tools become more accessible, consider integrating them into your operations.

AI can help with content creation, customer service, data analysis, and even personalized marketing, freeing up your time to focus on higher-level strategies.

- **Utilizing New Marketing Channels:** Be on the lookout for new platforms and marketing channels that align with your niche. Early adoption of emerging platforms can give you a competitive advantage and allow you to establish a strong presence before the market becomes saturated.

3. **Adapting to Algorithm Changes:**
   - **SEO Adaptation:** Search engine algorithms are constantly evolving, and staying ahead of these changes is crucial for maintaining your site's visibility. Regularly update your SEO strategies, optimize content for new ranking factors, and ensure your site remains compliant with the latest best practices.
   - **Social Media Algorithm Changes:**

Social media platforms frequently update their algorithms, which can affect your content's reach and engagement. Stay informed about these changes and adjust your social media strategies accordingly to maintain your audience's attention.

Avoiding Common Pitfalls

1. **Overcoming Burnout:**
    - **Maintaining a Healthy Work-Life Balance:** Running an online empire can be demanding, and it's easy to become overwhelmed. To avoid burnout, establish a healthy work-life balance by setting boundaries, delegating tasks, and taking regular breaks. Remember that sustainability requires long-term commitment, and preserving your mental and physical health is crucial to achieving this.
    - **Avoiding Overexpansion:**

While growth is important, expanding too quickly can lead to overextension and potential failure. Be strategic about scaling your business, ensuring that you have the necessary resources, team members, and infrastructure in place to support expansion.

2. **Ensuring Compliance and Transparency:**
    - **Adhering to Legal Requirements:** As your online empire grows, you'll need to navigate various legal and regulatory requirements, particularly concerning affiliate marketing disclosures, data privacy, and consumer protection. Ensure that your practices comply with relevant laws to avoid legal pitfalls.
    - **Transparency with Your Audience:** Maintain transparency in your affiliate marketing efforts by clearly disclosing affiliate links and being honest about your endorsements.

Building trust with your audience is essential for long-term success, and transparency is a key factor in establishing and maintaining that trust.

3. **Avoiding Content Stagnation:**
    - **Preventing Content Fatigue:** Repetitive or uninspired content can lead to audience disengagement. To avoid content stagnation, regularly infuse fresh ideas, perspectives, and creative approaches into your content strategy. Conduct audience surveys to understand their evolving interests and tailor your content to meet their needs.
    - **Updating Outdated Content:** As your niche evolves, some of your older content may become outdated. Regularly review and update your existing content to ensure it remains relevant and valuable. This not only keeps your audience informed but also improves your SEO performance.

Conclusion

Maintaining your online empire requires a combination of strategic planning, continuous learning, and adaptability. By implementing long-term strategies for sustained success, staying ahead of industry trends, and avoiding common pitfalls, you can ensure that your affiliate marketing and blogging efforts continue to thrive. Remember, building an empire is only the beginning—sustaining it requires dedication, foresight, and a commitment to excellence. With the right approach, your online empire can stand the test of time, delivering ongoing value to your audience and consistent rewards to you.

Chapter 15: Case Studies and Interviews

In this chapter, we will delve into real-world success stories, interviews with top bloggers and affiliate marketers, and case studies of successful affiliate marketing blogs. Learning from those who have already walked the path can provide invaluable insights and inspiration for your journey toward building and maintaining a thriving online empire.

Success Stories

Success stories offer a glimpse into the journeys of individuals who have turned their affiliate marketing and blogging efforts into highly successful online businesses. These stories highlight the challenges they faced, the strategies they implemented, and the milestones they achieved.

1. **Pat Flynn - Smart Passive Income:**
    - **Background:**

Pat Flynn started his online journey after being laid off from his job as an architect. He turned to the internet to generate income and soon discovered the power of affiliate marketing.

- **Strategy:** Pat built a blog around helping others achieve financial independence through passive income strategies. He created in-depth content, including podcasts, ebooks, and courses, while integrating affiliate links seamlessly into his content.
- **Results:** Pat's transparent and authentic approach to sharing his successes and failures resonated with his audience. Today, Smart Passive Income is one of the most recognized names in the online business world, generating significant revenue through affiliate marketing, online courses, and other income streams.

2. **Michelle Schroeder-Gardner - Making Sense of Cents:**
   - **Background:**

Michelle started her blog, Making Sense of Cents, as a hobby to track her financial journey. She quickly realized the potential of monetizing her blog through affiliate marketing.

- **Strategy:** Michelle focused on personal finance topics, providing actionable advice on saving money, paying off debt, and making extra income. She partnered with companies that aligned with her content and promoted their products and services through her blog and email marketing.
- **Results:** Michelle's blog grew rapidly, and she eventually quit her day job to focus on it full-time. She now earns a six-figure income each month, with a significant portion coming from affiliate marketing. Her success story has inspired countless others to pursue blogging as a full-time career.

3. **John Lee Dumas - Entrepreneurs on Fire:**
    - **Background:**

John Lee Dumas launched the podcast "Entrepreneurs on Fire" with the goal of interviewing successful entrepreneurs daily. He monetized his podcast through sponsorships and affiliate marketing.

- **Strategy:** John provided value-packed interviews that attracted a large audience of aspiring entrepreneurs. He strategically promoted affiliate products related to podcasting, online business, and entrepreneurship.
- **Results:** John's podcast quickly became a top-ranked business podcast, and his affiliate marketing efforts generated substantial income. His success has allowed him to create multiple income streams, including online courses, masterminds, and conferences.

Interviews with Top Bloggers and Affiliate Marketers

Interviews with successful bloggers and affiliate marketers provide direct insights from industry leaders who have achieved remarkable results. Their experiences, tips, and advice can serve as a guide for those looking to follow in their footsteps.

1. **Interview with Neil Patel:**
     - **Background:** Neil Patel is a digital marketing expert and the co-founder of several successful companies, including Crazy Egg, Kissmetrics, and Neil Patel Digital. He is also a prolific blogger and affiliate marketer.
     - **Key Insights:**
         - **On Content Creation:** Neil emphasizes the importance of consistently producing high-quality, in-depth content that addresses the needs of your audience. He believes that content should be both educational and actionable.

- **On SEO:** Neil is a strong advocate for mastering SEO to drive organic traffic. He advises bloggers to focus on long-tail keywords and building backlinks from reputable sources.
- **On Affiliate Marketing:** Neil shares that transparency and honesty are key when promoting affiliate products. He stresses the importance of only endorsing products that you genuinely believe in and that provide value to your audience.

2. **Interview with Harsh Agrawal:**
   - **Background:** Harsh Agrawal is the founder of ShoutMeLoud, a blog dedicated to helping bloggers and entrepreneurs succeed online. He is a leading voice in the affiliate marketing community.
   - **Key Insights:**
     - **On Niche Selection:**

Harsh highlights the importance of choosing a niche that you are passionate about and knowledgeable in. He believes that passion fuels persistence, which is critical for long-term success.

- **On Building Relationships:** Harsh emphasizes the value of building relationships with your audience and industry peers. He suggests engaging with your audience through comments, social media, and email newsletters to build trust and loyalty.
- **On Diversification:** Harsh advises against relying solely on affiliate marketing for income.

He suggests diversifying your revenue streams by exploring other monetization options, such as selling digital products, offering consulting services, and running sponsored content.

3. **Interview with Rosemarie Groner:**
    - **Background:** Rosemarie Groner is the founder of The Busy Budgeter, a blog that helps people manage their finances and create a balanced life. She has successfully turned her blog into a full-time business through affiliate marketing and other monetization strategies.
    - **Key Insights:**
        - **On Time Management:** Rosemarie shares that effective time management is crucial for balancing content creation, marketing, and monetization efforts. She recommends using tools like Trello and Asana to stay organized and productive.

- **On Affiliate Product Selection:** Rosemarie advises bloggers to choose affiliate products that solve specific problems for their audience. She believes that the most successful affiliate promotions are those that genuinely help people improve their lives.
- **On Scaling a Blog:** Rosemarie discusses the importance of scaling your blog by outsourcing tasks, automating processes, and expanding your content reach through guest posts and collaborations.

Case Studies of Successful Affiliate Marketing Blogs

Case studies provide a deep dive into the strategies and tactics used by successful affiliate marketing blogs. By analyzing these examples, you can gain insights into what works and how to apply similar strategies to your own blog.

1. **The Wirecutter:**
   - **Overview:** The Wirecutter, now owned by The New York Times, is a product review site that has built its reputation on providing detailed and unbiased reviews of consumer electronics and other products. The site earns revenue primarily through affiliate commissions.
   - **Strategy:** The Wirecutter's success is largely attributed to its commitment to thorough research and testing. The team behind the blog spends significant time testing products to provide readers with reliable recommendations. Their reviews are comprehensive, and they focus on creating value for the reader, which in turn builds trust.
   - **Results:** The Wirecutter has become one of the most respected product review sites on the internet, driving millions of dollars in affiliate sales each year.

Its model of in-depth, trustworthy reviews has been widely imitated, but few have achieved the same level of success.

2. **NerdWallet:**
    - **Overview:** NerdWallet is a personal finance website that helps consumers make informed financial decisions. The site offers comparisons of credit cards, loans, insurance, and other financial products, earning revenue through affiliate marketing.
    - **Strategy:** NerdWallet's success lies in its user-centric approach. The site offers a wealth of educational content, tools, and calculators that help users make informed decisions. By focusing on high-quality content and user experience, NerdWallet has built a loyal audience that trusts its recommendations.
    - **Results:**

NerdWallet has grown into a multimillion-dollar business, becoming a go-to resource for personal finance advice. Its affiliate marketing efforts are seamlessly integrated into the user experience, making it a model for monetizing content without compromising on value.

3. **This Is Why I'm Broke:**
    - **Overview:** This Is Why I'm Broke is a quirky affiliate marketing site that curates unique and unusual products from across the web. The site's playful tone and offbeat product selection have made it a hit with consumers looking for fun and creative gift ideas.
    - **Strategy:** The site focuses on viral content and social media sharing to drive traffic. Its success is built on a simple yet effective formula: find cool, unusual products and present them in a way that encourages impulse buying.

The site's design is clean and straightforward, with clear calls to action that drive affiliate sales.

- **Results:** This Is Why I'm Broke has become a popular destination for gift shopping, generating substantial affiliate revenue. Its success demonstrates the power of niche marketing and the appeal of a well-executed, unique concept.

Lessons Learned from the Pros

The insights and experiences of successful bloggers and affiliate marketers offer valuable lessons for anyone looking to build and sustain an online empire. Here are some key takeaways from the pros:

1. **Authenticity is Key:**
    - Whether you're creating content, promoting products, or engaging with your audience, authenticity is crucial.

Successful marketers like Pat Flynn and Michelle Schroeder-Gardner emphasize the importance of being genuine and transparent in all your interactions. Audiences can sense when you're being sincere, and this builds trust, which is the foundation of any long-term online business.

2. **Focus on Value:**
   - Providing value to your audience should be at the core of everything you do. From content creation to product recommendations, focus on helping your audience solve their problems and achieve their goals. Value-driven content not only attracts and retains readers but also increases the likelihood of conversions and repeat visits.

3. **Continuous Learning and Adaptation:**
   - The digital landscape is ever-changing, and staying ahead requires a commitment to continuous learning. Industry leaders like Neil Patel and Harsh Agrawal invest in ongoing education to stay updated on the latest trends and techniques.

They also emphasize the importance of being adaptable and willing to pivot when necessary.

4. **Diversification is Essential:**
    - Relying on a single income stream is risky. Successful bloggers and affiliate marketers diversify their income through multiple channels, including affiliate marketing, sponsored content, digital products, and consulting services. Diversification not only provides financial stability but also opens up new opportunities for growth.
5. **Data-Driven Decision Making:**
    - Leveraging data and analytics is a common theme among top performers in the industry. Understanding your audience's behavior, tracking key performance indicators, and optimizing your strategies based on data can significantly enhance your results. As John Lee Dumas and others have shown, data-driven decisions lead to more effective marketing and higher conversion rates.

Conclusion

This chapter has provided a deep dive into the real-world experiences of successful bloggers and affiliate marketers. By examining their journeys, strategies, and lessons learned, you can gain valuable insights that will help you build and maintain your own online empire. Remember, success in affiliate marketing and blogging is not just about following a formula; it's about finding your unique path, staying authentic, and continuously evolving in an ever-changing digital landscape. With the knowledge and inspiration gained from these case studies and interviews, you are well-equipped to take your online business to new heights.

Chapter 16: Conclusion

Your Path to Digital Dominance

Congratulations! You've made it to the final chapter of this comprehensive guide on building an online empire through affiliate marketing and blogging. As you reflect on everything you've learned, it's important to recognize that this journey is both exciting and challenging. The path to digital dominance is paved with continuous learning, experimentation, and perseverance. But with the right strategies, mindset, and dedication, you can turn your online ventures into a thriving and sustainable business.

In this concluding chapter, we'll recap the key strategies and insights covered in this book, provide some final words of encouragement, and outline the next steps you can take to propel your journey forward.

Recap of Key Strategies and Insights

Let's take a moment to revisit the core strategies and insights that will guide you on your path to success:

1. **Understanding Affiliate Marketing:**
   - You've learned the basics of affiliate marketing and how it can generate passive income. By understanding the mechanics of affiliate programs and how to choose the right products to promote, you're equipped to build a revenue stream that works for you around the clock.
2. **Blogging as a Business:**
   - Blogging is more than just sharing your thoughts; it's a powerful platform for building authority and connecting with your audience. By integrating affiliate marketing into your blog, you can create a business that offers value to readers while generating income.
3. **Laying a Strong Foundation:**

- Choosing the right niche and building a memorable brand are critical steps in your journey. By identifying profitable niches and developing a strong online presence, you set the stage for long-term success.

4. **Content is King:**
   - High-quality, value-driven content is the cornerstone of any successful online business. You've learned how to create content that engages and converts, and how to develop a content strategy that aligns with your goals.

5. **Mastering SEO and Building Traffic:**
   - Search engine optimization (SEO) is essential for driving organic traffic to your blog. By mastering both on-page and off-page SEO techniques, as well as leveraging social media and paid advertising, you can attract a steady stream of visitors to your site.

6. **Monetization Strategies:**

- From affiliate marketing to diversifying income streams through sponsored posts, ads, and product creation, you've explored various ways to monetize your blog. Understanding these strategies allows you to maximize your earnings potential.

7. **Maximizing Conversion Rates:**
   - Conversion optimization is key to turning visitors into customers. By crafting compelling calls-to-action, utilizing email marketing, and analyzing data, you can refine your strategies to boost conversions.

8. **Scaling and Automating:**
   - As your business grows, scaling and automating processes become crucial. Expanding your content, outsourcing tasks, and leveraging automation tools will help you manage growth while maintaining quality.

9. **Advanced Techniques and Maintaining Your Empire:**

- Leveraging data and exploring advanced marketing channels will help you stay ahead of the competition. Long-term success requires staying up-to-date with industry trends, avoiding common pitfalls, and continuously adapting your strategies.
10. **Learning from the Pros:**
    - The case studies and interviews with top bloggers and affiliate marketers provided real-world examples of what's possible. Their stories offer valuable lessons and inspiration as you embark on your own journey.

Encouragement for Your Journey Ahead

Building an online empire is not a sprint; it's a marathon. There will be challenges, setbacks, and moments of doubt along the way. But remember, every successful entrepreneur started where you are now—with a vision, determination, and a willingness to put in the work.

As you continue your journey, keep these principles in mind:

- **Stay Patient and Persistent:** Success doesn't happen overnight. It takes time to build an audience, gain trust, and see significant results. Stay committed to your goals, and don't be discouraged by slow progress.
- **Be Adaptable:** The digital landscape is constantly evolving. Stay open to new ideas, embrace change, and be willing to pivot your strategies when necessary. Adaptability is a key trait of successful entrepreneurs.
- **Focus on Value:** Always prioritize providing value to your audience. When you focus on helping others, success will naturally follow. Build relationships, engage with your audience, and listen to their needs.
- **Celebrate Small Wins:** Every milestone, no matter how small, is a step forward. Celebrate your achievements along the way and use them as motivation to keep going.
- **Keep Learning:**

- The more you learn, the more you grow. Stay curious, invest in your education, and continually seek out new knowledge to improve your skills and strategies.

Final Thoughts and Next Steps

As you reach the end of this book, you're not just closing a chapter—you're opening the door to endless possibilities. You now have the tools, knowledge, and strategies to build your own online empire. The next steps are up to you.

Here's a roadmap to guide your next steps:

1. **Take Action:** Start implementing the strategies you've learned. Whether it's setting up your blog, creating content, or joining affiliate programs, take the first step and keep moving forward.
2. **Set Clear Goals:** Define what success looks like for you. Set specific, measurable, achievable, relevant, and time-bound (SMART) goals to keep yourself focused and motivated.

3. **Build Your Network:** Connect with other bloggers, marketers, and entrepreneurs. Networking can open doors to new opportunities, collaborations, and valuable insights.
4. **Measure and Adjust:** Continuously monitor your progress, analyze data, and adjust your strategies as needed. Be willing to experiment and learn from both successes and failures.
5. **Stay Inspired:** Keep reading, learning, and seeking inspiration. Follow industry leaders, attend webinars, and stay engaged with the community to fuel your passion and drive.

Remember, the journey to digital dominance is uniquely yours. Embrace the challenges, savor the successes, and keep pushing forward. The online world is full of opportunities, and with the knowledge and strategies you've gained, you're well on your way to achieving your goals.

Here's to your success and the exciting journey ahead—your online empire awaits!

Chapter 17: Appendices

Resource List

As you embark on your journey to build and scale your online empire, having the right resources at your fingertips is crucial. This chapter provides a comprehensive list of recommended tools, platforms, reading materials, courses, and communities that will support you every step of the way. Whether you're just starting or looking to enhance your existing strategies, these resources will help you achieve your goals more efficiently and effectively.

Recommended Tools and Platforms

1. **Blogging Platforms:**
    - **WordPress.org:** The most popular self-hosted blogging platform, offering complete control and customization options.
    - **Squarespace:** A user-friendly, all-in-one platform with beautiful templates and integrated e-commerce options.

- **Blogger:** A simple, free platform for beginners who want to start blogging quickly.

2. **Domain and Hosting Services:**
   - **Bluehost:** Affordable hosting with a free domain name for the first year, perfect for WordPress users.
   - **SiteGround:** Known for excellent customer service, speed, and security features.
   - **Namecheap:** Offers affordable domain registration and hosting services with user-friendly interfaces.

3. **Content Creation and Management Tools:**
   - **Grammarly:** A powerful grammar and spell-check tool that enhances your writing quality.
   - **Canva:** A versatile design tool for creating blog graphics, social media posts, and more.
   - **CoSchedule:** A content calendar tool that helps you plan, schedule, and optimize your content.

4. **SEO Tools:**

- **Yoast SEO:** A popular WordPress plugin for optimizing your blog posts for search engines.
- **Ahrefs:** A comprehensive SEO toolset for keyword research, competitor analysis, and backlink tracking.
- **Google Analytics:** A free tool for tracking website traffic, user behavior, and other key metrics.

5. **Email Marketing Platforms:**
    - **Mailchimp:** A user-friendly platform offering email marketing, landing pages, and automation features.
    - **ConvertKit:** Designed specifically for creators, with advanced tagging and automation capabilities.
    - **AWeber:** A reliable email marketing tool with easy-to-use templates and robust analytics.

6. **Affiliate Marketing Networks:**
    - **Amazon Associates:** One of the largest and most accessible affiliate programs, offering a wide range of products.

- **ShareASale:** A popular affiliate network with a variety of merchants and products to promote.
- **CJ Affiliate:** Another leading affiliate network with diverse offers and reliable tracking.

7. **Social Media Management Tools:**
   - **Buffer:** A simple tool for scheduling and managing social media posts across multiple platforms.
   - **Hootsuite:** A comprehensive social media management platform with analytics, scheduling, and monitoring features.
   - **Tailwind:** A tool specifically designed for Pinterest and Instagram scheduling, offering smart automation features.

8. **E-commerce Platforms:**
   - **Shopify:** A leading e-commerce platform for setting up online stores, integrated with numerous payment gateways.
   - **WooCommerce:**

A customizable, open-source e-commerce plugin for WordPress, ideal for online shops.

- **Etsy:** A marketplace for handmade, vintage, and unique items, with built-in tools for sellers.

Essential Reading and Online Courses

1. **Books:**
    - **"The Lean Startup" by Eric Ries:** A must-read for entrepreneurs, offering a framework for developing successful businesses.
    - **"Crushing It!" by Gary Vaynerchuk:** Insights from one of the top influencers on how to build a personal brand and succeed online.
    - **"Influence: The Psychology of Persuasion" by Robert Cialdini:** A classic on the principles of persuasion, essential for marketers and bloggers.
2. **Online Courses:**

- **Coursera:** Offers courses on digital marketing, SEO, content creation, and more, taught by experts from leading institutions.
- **Udemy:** A vast library of courses on blogging, affiliate marketing, web development, and other relevant topics.
- **Skillshare:** A platform with creative and business courses, ideal for learning design, writing, and marketing skills.

3. **Blogs and Websites:**
    - **Neil Patel's Blog:** A treasure trove of actionable advice on SEO, content marketing, and digital strategy.
    - **ProBlogger:** A blog focused on helping bloggers turn their passion into a profitable business.
    - **Smart Passive Income:** Pat Flynn's site, filled with tips, tools, and case studies on affiliate marketing and online business.

Communities and Networks for Support

1. **Online Forums and Groups:**
   - **Reddit (r/Entrepreneur, r/Blogging, r/AffiliateMarketing):** Active communities where you can ask questions, share experiences, and learn from others.
   - **Warrior Forum:** A large online community dedicated to digital marketing and entrepreneurship.
   - **DigitalMarketer Engage:** A private Facebook group where digital marketers share tips, strategies, and experiences.
2. **Networking Groups:**
   - **Meetup.com:** Find local meetups and networking events for bloggers, marketers, and entrepreneurs.
   - **LinkedIn Groups:** Join professional groups related to blogging, affiliate marketing, and online business for networking and knowledge-sharing.
   - **Blogging Communities (BlogEngage, Triberr):** Platforms where bloggers can connect, share content, and support each other's growth.

3. **Mentorship and Coaching:**
   - **SCORE:** A free mentoring service for small business owners, offering guidance on all aspects of starting and growing a business.
   - **Mastermind Groups:** Consider joining or forming a mastermind group with like-minded entrepreneurs for mutual support and accountability.
   - **Online Coaching Platforms (Clarity.fm, Coach.me):** Connect with experienced coaches who can provide personalized advice and strategies.

Final Thoughts

Equipped with these resources, you're now ready to take your online business to the next level. Whether you're just starting or looking to scale, the tools, platforms, books, courses, and communities listed here will support your efforts and help you navigate the complex landscape of digital marketing, blogging, and affiliate marketing.

Remember, success in building an online empire is not just about the knowledge you acquire—it's about how you apply it. Use these resources to enhance your skills, stay informed, and connect with others who share your goals. As you continue on your journey, keep learning, experimenting, and growing, and you'll be well on your way to achieving digital dominance.

www.ingramcontent.com/pod-product-compliance
Lightning Source LLC
Chambersburg PA
CBHW052150220526
45471CB00004B/1613